STRATEGIC QUALITY POLICY FOR HIGHER EDUCATION

VIJAYA DESHMUKH

ATLANTIC

PUBLISHERS & DISTRIBUTORS (P) LTD

ATLANTIC
PUBLISHERS & DISTRIBUTORS (P) LTD
7/22, Ansari Road, Darya Ganj, New Delhi
Tel.: +91-11-4077 5252, 2327 3880
E-mail: orders@atlanticbooks.com
Web: www.atlanticbooks.com

Published by Atlantic Publishers & Distributors (P) Ltd 2024

Disclaimer

- The author and the publisher have taken every effort to the maximum of their skill, expertise and knowledge to provide correct material in the book. Even then if some mistakes persist in the content of the book, the publisher does not take responsibility for the same. The publisher shall have no liability to any person or entity with respect to any loss or damage caused, or alleged to have been caused directly or indirectly, by the information contained in this book.
- The author has fully tried to follow the copyright law. However, if any work is found to be similar, it is unintentional and the same should not be used as defamatory or to file legal suit against the author.
- If the readers find any mistakes, we shall be grateful to them for pointing out those to us so that these can be corrected in the next edition.
- All disputes are subject to the jurisdiction of Delhi courts only.

Printed & bound in India by Atlantic Print Services

Preface

The essence of quality assurance is to strive for excellence and continuous improvement. It is a comprehensive approach that encompasses every aspect of achieving greatness through ongoing enhancements. Absolute quality is achieved through a series of continuous improvement activities, involving all individuals who take ownership of their respective responsibilities and strive to enhance performance at every level.

In the era of globalization and increased student mobility between institutions and nations, it becomes imperative to ensure that students' qualifications are of high standards and universally recognized and respected. Education plays a crucial role in the economic and social development of a country, and this fact holds true for India, as well. As an emerging economy, India's progress greatly relies on the advancement and growth of its educational sector.

Higher education is a key driver of competitiveness and employment generation. It plays a crucial role in fostering excellence, expertise and knowledge, which leads to overall economic development. As a result, there is a universal need for well-defined strategies to promote and enhance higher education in virtually every country across the globe. A well-crafted and comprehensive approach to higher education paves the way for efficiency, leadership and success, serving as the primary basis to evaluate performance.

Strategic Quality Policy for Higher Education aims to enhance the effectiveness and organization of higher education, making it accessible to the general public while producing a committed, dedicated and expert human resource to contribute to the country's growth. This objective can be achieved by integrating high standards into the higher education framework.

This study presents a detailed examination of the Quality Assurance Systems (QAS) employed by different countries to enhance the effectiveness of procedures related to the induction of students, teaching methodologies, learning approaches, evaluation practices, student engagement, mentoring, etc. The focus is primarily on the elaborate, systematic, and comprehensive systems developed by the Quality Assurance Agency in the United Kingdom. The study covers the period from 2016 to 2018.

I would like to express my gratitude to the Indian Council for Social Science Research (ICSSR) for their invaluable support throughout this study. Additionally, I extend my thanks to the Quality Assurance Agency, UK, for providing valuable guidance that has been instrumental in shaping this research.

Vijaya Deshmukh

Contents

List of Tables

List of Figures

1
Introduction

1.1 TOWARDS QUALITY EDUCATION

Quality Assurance in an education institute is a process of continuous improvement including self-evaluation, benchmarking and external monitoring. It encompasses all phases of education from Induction of Students, Teaching & Learning, Evaluations, Student Engagement, and Mentoring to Accreditation. The British Standard Institution (BSI) defines quality as "the totality of features and characteristics of a product or service that bear on its ability to satisfy stated or implied needs" (BSI, 1991). The four approaches identified by Green and Harvey (1993) to define quality are being exceptional, consistency, fitness for purpose, value for money and being transformative.

Skills and knowledge relevant to employment must be central to the curriculum. The ability to think critically, perspectives about society and scientific understanding of nature are somewhere between distractions and unaffordable luxuries. Education should aim to foster and enable important abilities—the ability to think analytically and critically, to synthesize, to reflect, to have curiosity, to learn, etc.

Tenacity, willingness to take risk, integrity, initiative, empathy and so on is all shaped in a complex manner through life. Education should have relevance to the social milieu. If we want to build a diverse society with deep commitment we need to continuously discover and invent newer models of education that are adequately pragmatic or vice versa. There are no simple, easy or quick solutions.

There is a great stress on quality consciousness in education system. Quality may relate to a programme or an institution or the education system. Academic Audit is the process by which an institution can monitor its own academic standards and acts to assure and enhance the quality of its offering. Participation of students at various levels including delivery of courses, curriculum development and evaluation may set the process towards quality enhancement in education; perhaps the students are adequately equipped with the latest tools. Everyone agrees that the quality of Higher Education (HE) will play a key role in India's quest to emerge as a major world power. Almost half of the country's population is below 25 years. Almost 10% of them or 12 crore are between 18-23 ages. If they are equipped with both knowledge and skills, they could drive India's entrepreneurial and competitive spirit and make it into a global power. The quality of India's HE system will determine the pace of the country's emergence as a global power. A highly over-regulated system results in interference by multiple agencies which tend to stifle innovation and creativity, increase inefficiency and breed corruption and malpractices. An under-regulated system encourages exploitation, contributes to disorder and erosion of social justice. Therefore, it is important to design a balanced and all-encompassing regulatory mechanism that is overarching, transparent and ensures accountability, according to the Yash Pal report.

Students as the prime stakeholders, hold the highest stake in enhancing the quality of teaching and learning processes. Their entire future will be at stake if the education system does not prepare them adequately for the emerging situation in life. Starting as learners, they continue to sustain an emotional bond with their institutions, provided their experiences during the learning phase were fulfilling. They would cherish the fond memories of their learning. On the other hand, they would like to forget their experiences in a poor quality institution as a bad dream. Evaluation methods play a vital role in the career of students. The most important characteristic for any successful evaluation method is validity— whether a procedure measures what it purports to measure. It becomes inappropriate, meaningless, and useless to make specific inferences from invalid measurements. Successful evaluation methods also must be reliable, effective and efficient. Also, students should perceive the system as fair and equitable, rewarding them proportionately for their achievements. Moreover, in India majority of graduates and postgraduates available have low employability skills. No soft skills are included for career development and there is limited scope for value-based education which is a dire need for building up a socially responsible society. Student feedback is not a common practice and even if it is done, the same is not utilized effectively. The knowledge expansion is so rapid and the need to catch up with the pace of development is imminent.

Enhancing quality is a holistic process. The synergetic relationship among the students, teachers, management, parents, public, government and the production system are essential to achieve an enduring multiplier effect on quality enhancement. Isolated efforts in improving the quality of a few selected components of the education system such as the infrastructure, teacher training, research and funding or industry participation would be of limited value. Quite often the wholesome participation of students is neglected in favour of other components. Bringing students to the core of the quality enhancement process would stimulate the synergy with all the other components.

Negative perceptions arise of the institutions by the students due to many different reasons like, rigidity of the curricular framework, contents pedagogy and grading and feedback. Negative perceptions arise when students who have healthy aspirations and who can easily compare their experiences with better institutions, feel frustrated by their inability to improve the quality of the academic framework. It was highlighted that victimization and exploitation of students by institutions generates a sense of anger and disgust among some students and many of them succumb to immoral behaviour as a normal way of life.

The employers prefer institutions that have demonstrable academic quality along with value adding activities involving the students. Those students who have participated in the institutional quality processes are able to make rational career choices and the performance of such students in facing interviews and placement exhibit higher degree of self-confidence and maturity. Therefore, it is imperative that every institution makes an effort to associate students in their quality enhancement process going beyond a ritualistic approach.

Quality can be gauged in terms of relevance of the course curriculum to the galloping global changes, teacher quality, teaching techniques, teacher-student ratio and the demand for courses to be offered by the institution. Quality of education depends upon the overall academic environment of the institution and employability. Quality education can be achieved only if teachers take on the role of mentors to help bring out the best in a student. Teachers should be subject to lifelong learning so that outdated notes and syllabus are not carried over the years. Globalization and the need for education to meet global needs is desired.

The education sector is generating a lot of interest. Foreign players and private equity funds are aggressively looking at education sector for investment opportunities. The driving force behind the 21st-century economy is said to be education. The priority of policy makers today too is education and the concern about the employability and skills of the workforce. Long-term interests of the industry hinge on the quality of talent produced in the country. Industry must sponsor students and fund research in universities to increase their visibility. Education should not be de-linked from the needs of the industry. The concepts of creativity, collaboration, complex process of inquiry, critical thinking and communication need to be inculcated in the learning system. Investment in education and development of the human capital will ensure prosperity. Education should aim to produce responsible citizens embedded with humanism. The focus is on education for profitability, enrichment and generation of wealth and rarely on humanism, imagination and critical faculties, which are crucial to the welfare of humankind. The concept of a link between education and an inclusive citizenship has a special urgency in today's time.

The concepts of quality include quality as absolute, quality as relative, quality as a process and quality as culture. quality as culture gives an organizational view of quality as a process of transformation where each entity is important. There is considerable discussion and debate on autonomy of educational institutions. But very little attention has been paid to governance in these institutes. In modern times, the governance of universities should adopt modern and tested systems, which are robust. Performance challenges like attendance, learning outcomes, performance orientation, student employability, etc. remain unsolved.

The success of Total Quality Management in Higher Education requires in addition to patience, participatory management among well trained and educated partners as well as involvement, understanding and believes in the principles of TQM. It is difficult to state implicitly that TQM has been successfully implemented in the field of higher education as compared to the other industrial and service sectors. The implementation of TQM principles has not been encouraging but unless more of these principles are vigorously introduced in the field of higher education, it will be difficult to achieve a higher level of excellence in educational institutions. In this globalised world, if education is to scale new heights, institutions will have to accept the challenges and recognize that TQM values are as crucial in the field of education as in other management sectors where they have been successfully implemented with profound results.

If Higher Education has to move ahead, the strategy of its management needs to change. Education, a problem-solving instrument has become a problem-generating mechanism. The system should have been functional to national development. If we do not attend to the ills of the institutions in the system of higher education now, it may spark off, sooner than we think, a major national disaster. For this it is necessary to redefine the objective of higher education, make it an instrument of producing trained competence with sharpened problem-solving capability. It is desirable to have an annual auditing of the academic accomplishments and financial management of each university to take corrective measures.

Over a decade ago, management guru, Peter Drucker, had declared, "The knowledgable society will become far more competitive than any society we have yet known. There will be no poor countries; there will be only ignorant countries." Thus, the competitive position of every country will depend on the ability to harness and capitalize on knowledge. Knowledge is now driving the global economy, growth, wealth creation and prosperity. With almost half of the country's population below 25 years, the quality of India's HE system will determine the pace of the country's emergence as a global power. India is at threshold of becoming a global power and academic quality is very relevant. How well the university supports you in your learning: the teaching, the support available, how you are assessed, and the resources available determine quality. Quality is about setting and maintaining threshold academic standards, assuring and enhancing academic quality and providing information about higher education. Quality assurance is ultimately all about raising standards and ensuring students have the best possible experience at university.

There is, in fact, plenty that can be done even within the existing pattern of education and academic and professional course content to raise the level of awareness and proficiency of the students, provided the 'temples of learning and scholarship' live up to that description.

1.2 SCOPE AND OBJECTIVES

Up till now, some researchers have studied the working of universities. The previous research studies emphasized mostly on comparison between universities with reference to educational growth, developed and undeveloped geographic area, percentage of literacy, etc. The literature is yet to develop a theoretical and empirical base to understand the factors that contribute to quality education. Research conducted in this direction is highly specific to the Western countries and very few. Although some researchers have attempted to see the influence of certain aspects on quality of education, yet a comprehensive study related to quality education needs further exploration. There are many publications related to quality in higher education in parts, but what is required is a holistic approach to quality assurance and enhancement, taking into consideration all the stakeholders and proposing a quality policy which will finally enhance student experience and learning.

The objectives are:

- To evaluate programme development mechanisms, information provision, inducting and engaging students, inclusivity, teaching and learning, evaluation, student engagement, assessment and accreditation mechanism in different parts of the world, regulatory and governance mechanisms, student feedbacks, mentoring, sustainability, creative courses, etc. for HE.
- To find out whether the quality assurance mechanisms for HE are able to place adequate checks and balances, prevent manipulation and ensure quality of education and helps in employment generation. To find out whether governance mechanisms for HE ensure adequate learning and quality dissemination of education. To find out whether the feedback mechanism indicates enhanced student experience, meeting student's needs and value addition.
- Equipping graduates with skills for employment is just as important as supporting continuous professional development, up-skilling and re-skilling. To study whether HE meets the needs of students and employers alike.
- Strengthen links between HE provider, professionals, statutory and regulatory bodies, and encourage employers to contribute.
- Enhancement of student learning experience and internationalization.
- The purpose of the study is to organize some of the views about HE quality assurance and to present a possible path forward to enable HE leaders, policy

makers, and the students to achieve their common goal of improving the success of the sector.

- To find out whether the assessment is able to measure the quality of the institute. This will help to find the deficient areas, if any, and give an idea to remove these deficiencies or to prepare for present and future requirements. It will help the institutes to review their systems for better efficiency in case of any loopholes.
- To give a new insight to the assessment process and identify areas that are vital in determining the quality of the institute. The present study will help institutes to understand and adopt better policies and practices while performing their regular duties.
- To propose effective mechanisms for quality assurance in vital areas such as developing a new programme, teaching learning, adding creative and innovative courses, evaluation, student engagement, feedback, and mentoring, inclusive and sustainable literacy.

The overall objectives are:

- Education should meet students' needs and be valued by them.
- Safeguard standards in an increasingly diverse environment and international context.
- Drive improvements in HE.
- Improve public understanding of HE standards and quality.

1.3 RESEARCH METHODOLOGY

The research proceeds as follows. It begins with an overview of the accreditation system and other quality assurance mechanisms for HE, including their history, processes, and shortcomings. Reviewing how some recent efforts to improve quality assurance that emphasize performance-based assessment have sought to overcome some of these shortcomings, but, ultimately, poorly accommodate institutional diversity and do little to support improvement in management-based regulation. Conclude by elaborating on broad design principles for reforming the HE quality assurance system to make it more rigorous, consistent, and supportive of innovation, improvement and sustainable.

It includes library and online research on topics related to quality education and accreditation. It also involves conceptual study, personal observation, experiences and interaction with the stakeholders, making use of the web to build first-hand information for future analysis. The rationale is to find out approaches and practices that can be adopted to generate innovative practices for quality education. The study relies on a combination of research methodologies. Specifically, two phases were included in the research design. The first phase involved a review of what are the measures for quality assurance and how different countries and institutions are handling it. The second phase involved experts, administrators and stakeholders of institutions in addressing the issues and how they can be assessed. Personal experiences and observations while visiting various institutions are recorded. Inductive approach was used to describe phenomenon and generate theory.

Few research questions are given below:

- Whether the HE institutions are providing adequate, valid, reliable, useful and accessible information about their provision?
- Whether the governance mechanisms ensure quality teaching, reliable evaluation and measurement of learning outcomes, assessments and certifications?
- Whether creative and innovative courses are offered?
- Whether inclusive practices are followed?
- Whether feedback mechanism exists for students? Whether the feedback is analyzed properly to improve systems and processes and enhances student experience?
- Whether students are involved in decision making? Whether there is improvement through self-reflexive criticism?

- Whether the accreditation and assessment body ensures enhancement of knowledge, learning and quality of the education? Whether they can ensure upholding of quality and standards?
- Whether the regulatory body ensures checks and balances on Higher Education Institutions (HEIs)? Whether the grants are linked to learning and quality provisions?
- Whether there is proper mentoring and addressal of grievances?
- Whether the sustainability goals are achieved leading to sustainable literacy?

1.4 NATURE AND SCOPE

- To study the programme design procedures, information provisions, inducting and engaging students, teaching and learning, evaluation, student engagement, assessment and accreditation mechanism in different parts of the world, regulatory and governance mechanisms, student feedbacks, mentoring, inclusiveness, sustainability, creative courses, etc. for HE.
- To study whether the accreditation and assessment mechanism for HE in India are able to place adequate checks and balances, prevent manipulation and ensure quality of education leading to employment generation. To study governance mechanisms and find out whether it is able to ensure adequate learning and quality dissemination of education. To study the feedback mechanism and if it indicates enhancing student experience, meeting student's needs and value addition.
- The study will be carried out at the national and international level. Efforts will be made to include as many educational institutions as possible to make the study more acceptable and relevant. Study will also include regulatory and assessment bodies like the MHRD, UGC, AICTE, NAAC, NBA, etc.

- To study efficient international standards for quality assurance.
- To propose efficient mechanisms to ensure quality education.

1.5 RESEARCH METHODS

The study is based on experimental type of research where researcher mainly intends to study, develop and ascertain the policies, strategies and processes for quality HE. This exercise involves study of the various aspects of institutions like the organization structure, operations, functions and management at all levels of administration and government policies, student feedback, regulatory mechanisms, quality assurance and enhancement mechanisms, etc.

A wide range of research methodologies will be used, namely:

- Literature review
- Survey research methods based on interviews
- Descriptive investigations
- Using secondary sources of data

An empirical study will be conducted to get feedback on various policies, strategies and processes observed in the HEIs. It is important for the researcher to find out whether they have helped in enhancing quality of education.

The proposed research consists of two parts, viz. surveys, direct interviews, telephonic interactions. The second part of the study consists of conceptual study including library research—referring to the important journals, periodicals, reports, publications and research volumes on HE and management, quality assurance manuals of various countries and making use of the web to build up first-hand information for future analysis. The results of the extensive library research and surveys are combined and suitable recommendations made to help in application of better policies, strategies and processes for quality assurance and enhancement in HE.

1.6 METHOD AND TOOLS OF DATA COLLECTION

The literature which was of particular use for generating research ideas is Quality Assurance Manuals of various countries, articles in academic and professional journals, reports, book chapters, books, etc. Of particular use were academic review articles. These articles contain both a considered review of the state of knowledge in that topic area and point towards areas where further research needs to be undertaken. Reports were also of use. The most recently published are usually up to date and, again, often contain recommendations that may form the basis of the research idea. Searching for publications was also undertaken. The most accessible and those of most likely use in showing how the research relates to that of other people were reports—research reports, government reports and academic reports, conference proceedings and theses—they are also a good source of further references.

The literature sources available to help develop a good understanding of and insight into previous research is divided into three categories—Primary (published and unpublished), Secondary and Tertiary.

Primary data was collected through structured, semi-structured and in-depth interviews and observation involving systematic observation, recording, description, analysis and interpretation of people's behaviour. Data regarding the information systems used by the organization has been collected by way of personal interviews with the top management and functional heads of the university. Other necessary information is gathered through discussions held with the persons working in various sections/departments and also by observation method.

Published data collected was used for study from libraries/ Internet. Various seminars and research papers, published and un-published material on Quality Assurance System, annual reports, manuals and journals of related work, on-line databases containing information were accessed via the Internet.

Secondary data—Organizations collect and store a variety of data to support their operations, which was assessed. On-line databases containing information were accessed via the Internet. Documentary secondary data including written documents such as notices, correspondence, minutes of meetings, reports, administrative and public records, speeches, etc. were included. Written documents like books, journals, and magazine articles and newspapers were used. Documentary secondary data including non-written documents such as DVDs and CDROMs were also accessed.

Tertiary literature sources, also called search tools, designed to help locate primary and secondary literature or to introduce a topic including indexes and abstracts as well as encyclopedias and bibliographies via Internet or held by library were seen. For this study, research materials have been collected from the libraries, Springer Link and IEEE digital libraries, ACM Digital Library, MHRD Consortia, Compact Disc Databases, CARS—computer-aided reference services. Out of the collected materials, over 500 reading materials, 15 theses, monographs, textbooks and quality assurance manuals of various countries, quality codes have been used for the study.

Information from the above departments was collected by a qualitative survey based on interviews with the respondents. In-depth face to face interviews with each respondent were planned in the places as suggested by them. These interviews were referred to as (i) preliminary—introductory interviews; (ii) follow-up interviews; and (iii) concluding interviews. The interview contained sections which were drawn from the conceptual framework of the study. Discussions were carried with various members of the departments to have a detailed know-how of the procedures. The time available with a particular respondent varied. Again, it was also essential to study some non-verbal behaviour of the respondents as being government offices some of the employees and citizens were not expected to tell all the facts truthfully. According to Bailey, an interview provides us with flexibility i.e., different questions with different respondents, observes non-verbal behaviour, and allows varying the order, variability of the time of interview.

1.7 RELEVANCE

The research is related to regulatory and governance mechanisms, student feedbacks, assessment and accreditation mechanisms, information provision, etc. for Indian HE. The study has national and international relevance and importance as it will give a direction for quality assurance and enhancement in a holistic manner in the Indian HE, which will also influence the students seeking admissions abroad and facilitate international collaborations. If effective systems are laid out relating to assessment of quality and standards, Indian education will be rated at a higher level and equivalent to international standards.

2
Literature Review

2.1 BOOKS REVIEWED

The Literature Review has been carried out to cover various aspects of quality enhancement in education. This, in short, is the review of the available literature on ensuring quality education in institutes of HE. All these studies and works undertaken by different authors and scholars have their own significance. Some more books and research papers can be added to the existing list. But to avoid repetition only few books, thesis and published research papers/articles and quality assurance systems of India, UK, Europe, Australia and USA have been reviewed by the researcher. Every publication has contributed something new and is related to some specific area. They have touched different aspects of the problem from different angles and as a result each study has contributed immensely to the subject.

2.1.1 Winds of Reform in Education

There is a remarkable growth in education access across all the states since Independence. The literacy rates have risen from 16.67% to 64.84%. Due to various policies, the enrolment in elementary education is improving; though lowering the dropout rate and improving the quality of learning remain a challenge. Learning assessments also show that the children who do remain in school are not learning the basics of literacy, numerics and skills required for all-round development. Population should be literate, employable and employed. There are 300 million Indians who are illiterate. Amartya Sen defined development as freedom because in the final analysis, an illiterate, unemployable or unemployed Indian is not a free India. A nation advances proportionately to education and awareness and intelligence spreads among masses.

Right to Education though landmark legislation has brought many challenges, which we will have to face and the greatest challenge is posed by the fast-growing population. A large number is still illiterate and is not aware of the importance of education for the upliftment of human life. All forms of employment and engagement, which hinder the development of child, should be banned. To bring sustainable change in the education sector, creating awareness among the general masses and intensive attitudinal transformation is required. Additionally, rational utilization of allotted resources and striving towards the goals with genuine commitment can only bring success. At the elementary level, universal access to quality, infrastructure and effectiveness of teaching are serious challenges. The learning outcomes cannot be guaranteed with RTE Act as there will be no certification through testing. Education will therefore only seem to have been delivered. Talking about quality seems out of question when we continue to struggle with embarrassing numbers, poor training, meagre salary, one-room structures that sometimes lack simple blackboards, no computers and playgrounds, an environment that repeals the students. The elementary education should imbibe in all children, the qualities essential of the vibrant and dynamic democracy, including value of tolerance, morality and compassion as well as the basic abilities of reading, writing, comprehension and reasoning.

Everything we do is about speed, scale, flexibility, etc. The future is all about what the kids understand on social networking, collaboration and teamwork; how we use the video and power of Internet, wired and wireless. Better Internet connectivity and equipment strengthen library resources and will have a positive impact on the quality in rural areas. When nearly all educationally developed countries attained their current educational status by legislating free and compulsory education, India has dithered and lagged behind in introducing such legislation. A beginning has been made, but a long and difficult road lies ahead for the Indian child.

India is at the crossroad of capacity and capability for HE. The intent of getting foreign universities into India may be to provide affordable quality education. The private education in India has been primarily within the control of politicians who seek on paper collaboration for a student certification. Research in Indian universities is not up to the mark. The entire HE today is driven for employability. So from the students' aspect, certification is important. While a good overseas degree would become a little more affordable for those who wish to pursue such degrees, some dubious foreign universities may try to exploit this opportunity to attract students, keen on a foreign degree. The government's open door to the West is being criticized for creating another special education zone which has the ability to harm the interests of the weaker sections and facilitate cut-throat competition. Allowing foreign universities in India should not give them a license to destroy the Indian institutions and education should not become a commodity.

Indian HE suffers from quality and relevance gap in comparison with developed countries. Indian universities need to bridge this gap and work towards developing an education hub by attracting reputed scholars in teaching and research. Foreign colleagues, just in the normal course of their functioning, will inspire the Indian counterparts.

2.1.2 Changing Governance and Quality Perspectives

Although the Indian Government is making considerable budgetary allocations for education expenditure, the quality of education still remains one of the major concerns. While the country is home to a considerable number of engineering, medical and management schools, the industry by and large suffers from the talent crunch. Ensuring access to quality education for all, in particular for the poor and rural population, is central to the economic and social development of India. Children and parents are clueless where to go when they're denied quality education.

Managing people is considered more of an art than science. A myriad of human variables interact. An educational leader may need basic skills like working together, understanding human behaviour, and vision for the future, motivation and development of key competencies. Some of the essential traits required in a leader are striving for excellence, communicating effectively, creativity, maintaining human relations and delegating efficiently. It is desirable to have an annual auditing of the academic accomplishments and financial management of each university to take corrective measures.

If an educational institution is committed to give high-quality education, it should be built on values and ethics and be innovative in offering its teaching programmes. High-quality education system should lay a strong foundation to "values" among students. Under such circumstances, it should look for individuals not only with intelligence and subject expertise but also with "missionary zeal". The quality of HE is based on four foundations—Relevance, Accountability, and Efficiency of the system and Equity.

The book consists of articles by experts on governance and financial management of universities, need for quality in Indian education, 'Talent Crunch' and improving content and delivery of education.

2.1.3 Education for Human Resource Development

A balance between liberal and instrumental education is necessary for a holistic social outcome. The basic purpose of education is to generate livelihood. Skills and knowledge relevant to employment must be central to the curriculum. The ability to think critically, perspectives about society and scientific understanding of nature are necessary and cannot be a luxury. Liberal education aims to foster and enable important abilities—the ability to think analytically and critically, to synthesize, to reflect, to have curiosity, to learn, etc. If we want to build a diverse society with deep commitment, we need to continuously discover and invent newer models of education that are adequately pragmatic or vice versa. The government policies should lay emphasizes on inclusive and equitable HE. This will call for conscious efforts to ensure that the achievement in HE does not suffer from disparities across region, gender, social groups such as scheduled castes, scheduled tribes, other backward castes, and minorities, physically challenged and economically deprived. The 11th Plan strategy for inclusion recognized three imbalances, namely inter-regional, inter-social group and gender. The plan proposed some measures to reduce these imbalances. It proposes support to universities and colleges located in districts having lower GER, opening of new colleges, with matching contribution from the states in 350 districts, with lower enrolment.

Rural-based universities can play a critical role in raising the literacy rate and building social capital; which increases prospects of employability and self-employment leading to high productivity and a higher GDP; higher standards of living and an improved quality of life and social well-being. The rural university should function like a catalyst to bring about needed changes in rural India and should be re-organized to meet the requirement of the community. It needs humane governance, organization and economic systems and a vigorous interface with the community for decisions, strategies and policies regarding education and allocation of resources. India consists of different religious groups, racial groups, cultural groups, linguistic groups, etc. All communities have their own way of life, occupation, morale and social and cultural system. All racial and cultural groups have their own pattern of lifestyle and behaviour. Protection of these unique cultures and patterns of life have become an important aspect of education. Education should protect, preserve and promote these unique cultures by introducing/implementing different plans and programmes and strategies. Education should have relevance to the social milieu, which changes overtime.

Development of a nation is directly related to the development of human resources and for adequate development of human resources there is a need for quality education. It is the process of increasing the capacity of human resource through development. Skills and knowledge, technology and research and inquiry are required for advancement. Exploring into the unknown or unfamiliar comes naturally to all living beings. Creativity and innovation, capacity to know and use latest technologies for aiding their learning process and to enhance their learning ability is necessary. The aptitude for entrepreneurship and taking calculated risk should be cultivated right from the beginning in the university environment. Leadership quality in the students is also necessary so that they are able to guide others in future. Life-long learning is necessary for wholesome and continuous development.

Economic progress and national development is directly related to knowledge growth since knowledge is power. Universities have to play vital role in knowledge generation, information processing and knowledge management, which also requires different types of expertise. Innovative approach essentially involves development of ideas and concepts, experimentation, interpreting the results and decisions. Tenacity, willingness to take risk, integrity, initiative, empathy and so on, are all shaped in a complex manner through life. Skill enhancement is receiving a lot of attention. The government has done well to launch a skill development programme that requires various departments, industry bodies, educational institutions and others to work together. The Prime Minister has recently appointed an advisor on skill development from the corporate world. The Finance Minister in his Budget speech of 2008-09 announced the formation of the National Skill Development Corporation mandate to provide skills training to 50 crore people by the year 2022.

As the country continues to expand its share of youth population with an expected average age of 29 years by the year 2020, it becomes imperative that we create a fertile environment with productive jobs for the youth. Now, with the appointment of a person from the corporate world to oversee skills development, there is a great hope and enthusiasm in achieving this target. Hope, this will overcome this daunting employability challenge and provide productive jobs to hundreds of millions of youth in the coming years. Technology is another buzzword for the education sector. Digital content providers create content database using a wide range of topics to assist teachers or tailer making lesson plans. Besides active teaching, additional skills such as personality development and value-based teaching are also being packaged. Use of e-readers and laptops by students is become more common, as the educational institutions get more computerised and automated with ERP systems.

There is considerable discussion and debate on autonomy of educational institutions. But very little attention has been paid to governance in these institutions. Experts have called for sweeping changes in the HE system and advocated shift towards adoption of a choice-based credit course along with semester system, promoting students' mobility within and outside the system, subjecting all faculty members to a review once every five years. A systematic system of assessment, accreditation and recognition for the institutions of HE and the degrees awarded is necessary to avoid confusion among students and to provide seamless mobility of the graduates of Indian universities to international educational institutions. The Prime Minister's advisory committee has favoured a specialist group of teachers to conduct examinations and evaluate students instead of the current practice of involving all teachers in setting question papers and checking answer sheets. Various measures for education reforms have been suggested by the advisory group to re-look at the present examination system including the system of final examinations, entrance examinations, qualifying examinations, and selection examinations. The examination should not be a source for harassment. All these are happy developments towards a hopeful bright future for education.

2.1.4 Education in Emerging India

The academic scenario has over the years undergone a tremendous change assuming new dimensions of modern perceptions of global realities. There is an advent of communication revolution and mass media information super highway. Globalization, increasing competition, decreasing funding, rapidly developing technology and socio-political multiplicity are stimulating changes which tend to redefine education. Quality system requires leadership, well-designed processes, diligent follow-up and continuous improvement. Quality is not about measuring or quantifying, it is about planning, visualizing and creativity. The size and complexity of institutes calls for rapid and efficient methods of planning, communication and analysis, individual creativity has to be maximized at all levels. There is an increasing pressure to rationalize the decision-making process, ensure better allocation of resources, increase accountability and ensure a transparent operation and evaluation of objectives. Internal monitoring through effective control of the components is required. In this direction, use of Information Technology can help analyze the interdependence of the different components of the system, and rationalize the decision-making and resource management by way of a better communication, feedback and control. Technology, globalization, migrations, multiculturalism, and shrinking borders combine to promote a more interdependent future, in which development of a global mind-set is necessary in order to live meaningfully and productively in the 21st century. One has to confront to ever-shifting social, cultural, and technological challenges.

Research is of immense importance for defining of excellence of HEIs and is considered an important parameter for the ranking of universities world-wide. It provides valuable revenue for funding. This is not happening in Indian HE and even important academic institutions are yet to make their mark globally as far as research is concerned. There is no national body instituted by the Indian Government to regularly evaluate the research performance of Indian universities/institutions. The accreditation process, at the same time, provides only 10% weightage to 'research'. This situation in India becomes even more complex due to global shifts in the research environment brought about by innovative research methods, new institutional complexities and the need for diverse criteria to evaluate research quality. With an increasing number of research participants and variety in research topics, single university systems are often unable to accommodate research requests. There needs to be a facilitating research system, based on centre-to-centre research, to accommodate and broaden the scope of research.

With the changing trends, one has to learn how to deal with unexpectedness, ambiguity and otherness as well as the resulting culture bumps or culture shock. The knowledge, skills and attitudes that are necessary for successful intercultural communication have to be observed, discussed and practiced. The rapid development requires a new way of living and learning together. This global mind-set can only result from competent intercommunication among people from diverse cultures. These dynamics strongly emphasize proficient intercultural competence. Developing intercultural competence is a concern for the HE. The need is to remain intellectually and culturally viable in a rapidly changing world, preparing students to vie competitively in the global environment, and staying informed with globalized knowledge. The internationalization of HE has become one possible response to such challenges. Institutions need to understand the importance of cross-cultural competence to ensure intercultural effectiveness. Many organizations are now realizing its importance. This helps deal effectively with differences in a positive manner.

A customer-service approach to the student-teacher relationship undermines effective pedagogy. It has led to decline of respect for teachers and perpetuation of a culture of complaint and cynicism. Educating students is more important than coddling them and treating them as customers. Consumerism in education also undermines the concept of merit. Teachers serve students in ways the students find pleasing. If business implies expense control, budgeting systems, focus on profits, more bureaucracy or more forms to fill out the triumph of administration over education, then it is to be dreaded. If, on the other hand, business implies greater teamwork, greater coordination, empowerment of the suppliers and recipients of education and relevant education, than it has to be embraced wholeheartedly. HE needs to be nobler than business and more decent and humane in the purpose it serves.

Education is the priority area where there is a growing need for Equal Opportunity Policy of inclusion and diversity. Information and web technology needs to be used to provide access to information both within and beyond the educational institution.

Education is a useful liberating force and agent of social change especially in developing countries. A large part of the empowerment process is associated with education of the women themselves. Poverty, illiteracy, and powerlessness are the major obstacles to women empowerment in developing countries. Women are deprived access to education in conventional system. Enrolment of women dwindles as they move up the educational hierarchy. The root of the problem is the degree of importance women themselves attach to education. Lack of personal ambition prevents women from thinking about pursuing educational goals. In the case of the working women in the cities, there has been a tendency to abandon further education because of the demands of work and family as well as the huge costs associated with pursuing higher studies in conventional systems. Educational planners need to understand that the knowledge-based society of the twenty-first century demands effective methods of dissemination of information/knowledge.

Due to limitations in resources; both human and financial, the traditional conventional approach of teaching can no longer satisfy the snowballing population. Open and Distance Learning has therefore come up as a realistic alternative to conventional education. It will benefit the persons with disabilities, and women, especially women with disabilities who are subject to double disadvantage due to barriers and discrimination "being treated less favourably when endeavouring to access educational resources". There is a need to encourage social change, promoting the role of sharing resources, information and power. There is a need for increased education support services for women, and persons with disabilities. Around 1500 universities across the country are needed to meet the demand in the next five years—almost five times the existing number. It is not possible for any government to run all the universities. It is important to design a balanced and all-encompassing regulatory mechanism that is overarching, transparent, and ensures accountability. Our real challenge lies in our ability to use technology, distance learning in an effective way to improve productivity, efficiency, reduce costs and improve access. Apart from the right to education we need to ensure that our institutions are modernized. It is about content, new courses and things that will lead to skills. Access to education will change the aspirations of the people.

2.1.5 Quality Assurance in HE

The philosophy of quality assurance (QA) and total quality management is derived from industrial and commercial practice. We propose the adoption of international standards ISO 9000 (used in industry and commerce) to higher educational institutions to assure and improve the quality, efficiency, and delivery of their programmes and services. This paper examines the scope and structure of a QA system applicable to educational institution. In particular, it looks at the requirements in terms of the objectives to be achieved, the procedures needed to be undertaken, and the necessary CAE tools and techniques for achieving improved QA in HE.

The QA techniques should be used to predict, monitor and verify efficiency of any investments or enhancements (new study program, CAL equipment and software, staff trainings) into educational processes. An example of a QA system adopted by one of the new UK universities is outlined as an illustration. The philosophy of quality assurance (QA) and total quality management (TQM) is derived from industrial and commercial practice. Adoption of international standards ISO 9000 (used in industry and commerce) is proposed to assure and improve the quality and efficiency of the educational process. The QA techniques should be used to predict, monitor and verify efficiency of any investments or enhancements (new study program, CAL equipment and software, staff trainings) into educational processes. Several CAE tools and techniques for quality improvement and for guidance in establishing and implementing a quality system are described.

The educational process will be seen as supplying knowledge (skills and understanding) for students—the customers. The customer is free to choose the suitable service provider (educational institution) and customer satisfaction is the most important factor for the commercial success of any service provider. The above philosophy is well understood by most of the new private educational establishments. In this paper we will discuss our proposed approach, indicating the scope and structure of a QA system for an entire institution. The paper specifies the requirements in terms of the objectives to be achieved, the procedures needed to be undertaken, and the necessary CAE tools and techniques for achieving improved QA in HE.

The introduction of QA methodology should be considered by all educational institutions. Contrary to quality control (testing the results), QA includes all activities needed to provide effective services for customers during the basic educational process and the full life cycle of the graduate (a graduate is a product of an educational institution). The official goals [see ISO 9000] of an educational institution should include:

- customer (student and his sponsor) satisfaction consistent with professional standards
- continuous improvement of service
- giving consideration to the requirements of industry, commerce and the public sector
- efficiency in providing the service.

On the other hand, this general description should be customised to a set of local quality objectives, according to the mission and circumstances of the educational institution:

- clear definition of customers' (the student and his sponsor) needs with appropriate quality measures
- preventive action and controls to avoid customer dissatisfaction
- optimising quality-related costs for the required performance and grade of service
- creation of collective commitment to quality within the educational organisation
- continuous (and never ending) review of service requirements and achievements to identify opportunities for service quality improvement.

2.1.6 Top-down Approach to Educational Quality System

Effective QA in large and complex organisations is beyond the capacity of individuals using informal methods. A systematic approach should be based on the requirements of the organisation as a whole rather than the needs of local subsystems. This means that a top-down approach starting from the overall mission, vision and strategy of the institution must be taken.

Responsibility for detailed planning and operation of procedures is devolved to academic units (chairs, departments, units), giving them freedom to define and use methods appropriate to their own disciplines. It may happen that existing structures and systems should be changed in the light of the agreed objectives. Objectives at the local level should ensure that the overall quality is maintained and improved. Support and administration quality plan. Each supporting and administrative function within the unit which has an impact on the quality of education, should prepare a quality plan including local objectives, procedures, performance indicators as well as structure, responsibility and review mechanisms. The academic unit quality plan should also be specified in the same manner as the support and administration quality plan.

The new study programme should be validated using officially approved validation procedures and probably a final validation meeting of educational staff and other bodies involved in preparation of the programme. Once the objectives are agreed, the proper activities should be defined and documented.

2.1.7 Quality Systems and Procedures

A formalised and documented system of QA (as described in the ISO 9000 family of standards) should be designed and developed. For all parts of the educational institution structure (e.g. central administration, academic units, support and administrative services), the relevant activities should be proposed, based on the agreed aims and objectives. A review and audit process carried out on all levels is an integral part of the concept. For quality improvement to be successful, senior management must encourage and motivate the staff and implement their recommendations whole-heartedly. Many industrial organisations have failed to implement effective quality programmes because proposals from staff were not adopted.

To achieve the quality objectives, the highest level of management should establish a quality system with a structure for effective control, evaluation and improvement of service quality. To ensure that critical tasks are not neglected, responsibility for key activities should be assigned to specified staff. The responsibility and authority defined should be consistent with the means and methods necessary for achieving the objectives. However, involvement, commitment and effective collaborative working of all personnel is essential.

Audits should be planned and evaluated on a regular basis to determine if the activities and related results comply with planned arrangements. The audit should include [see ISO 9000]:

- scheduling activities and areas to be audited
- assignment of personnel with appropriate qualifications to conduct audits
- documented procedures for carrying out audits, including:
  - recording and reporting results
  - reaching agreement on corrective actions taken on the deficiencies found during the audit
  - observations, conclusions and suggestions.

Personnel conducting the audit should be independent of those having direct responsibilities in the areas being audited.

2.2 THE UK QUALITY CODE FOR HIGHER EDUCATION

The role of the Quality Assurance Agency (QAA) is to safeguard the standards of HE in the UK and to work towards enhancing the quality of students' learning opportunities. Following extensive consultation across the sector, the QAA has fully revised its guidance to institutions in the form of the UK Quality Code of HE. The Quality Assurance Agency (QAA) sets out the UK Quality Code for HE. This replaced the previous academic infrastructure from the 2012-13 academic years. The UK Quality Code for HE (the Quality Code) is used to assure the standards and quality of UK HE. It has been developed and is maintained by the Quality Assurance Agency for HE

(QAA) through consultation with the HE sector. Individual HE providers use the Quality Code to ensure students have a high quality educational experience. It consists of a general introduction and a series of separate chapters grouped in three parts. It is published online at www.qaa.ac.uk/qualitycode. Threshold academic standards are the minimum acceptable level of achievement that a student has to demonstrate to be eligible for the award of academic credit or a qualification. For equivalent qualifications, the threshold level of achievement is agreed across the UK.

Academic standards are the standards that individual degree-awarding bodies set and maintain for the award of their academic credit or qualifications. These may exceed the threshold academic standards. They include the standards of performance that a student needs to demonstrate to achieve a particular classification of a qualification. Academic quality refers to how and how well the HE provider supports students to enable them to achieve their award. It covers learning, teaching and assessment, and all the different resources and processes a provider puts in place to help students progress and fulfil their potential. QA is the process for checking that the academic standards and quality of HE provision meet agreed expectations.

The Quality Code provides a set of nationally agreed expectations that all UK HE providers are required to meet. It informs the learning and teaching activities of HEIs, from foundation level to postgraduate research degrees. The code relates to all aspects of the student lifecycle and their experience of HE and therefore on the work of all academic staff who are engaged in teaching. The QAA works with the HE sector to develop maintain and update the Quality Code. HE providers apply the Quality Code in designing and delivering their programmes of study. The Quality Code will be of most importance to those staff who is involved in setting and maintaining academic standards and quality enhancement.

The Quality Code comprises three parts as follows:

Part A: Setting and maintaining academic standards

Part B: Assuring and enhancing academic quality

Part B includes the following chapters:

Chapter B1: Programme design, development and approval

Chapter B2: Recruitment, selection and admission to HE

Chapter B3: Learning and teaching

Chapter B4: Enabling student development and achievement

Chapter B5: Student engagement

Chapter B6: Assessment of students and the recognition of prior learning

Chapter B7: External examining

Chapter B8: Programme monitoring and review

Chapter B9: Academic appeals and student complaints

Chapter B10: Managing HE provision with others

Chapter B11: Research degrees.

Part C: Information about HE provision

Each chapter sets an overarching expectation for the particular area. This is followed by a series of indicators, which highlight sound practice and include examples of how each indicator may be met. Universities and colleges, whatever their source of funding, and other organisations involved in the delivery of UK HE programmes are known collectively as HE providers. The Quality Code sets out the formal expectations that all UK HE providers reviewed by QAA are required to meet. It is the nationally agreed, definitive point of reference for all those who deliver or support UK HE programmes. The code gives individual HE providers guidelines for:

- setting and maintaining the academic standards of their HE programmes and awards;

- assuring the quality of the learning opportunities they provide for students.

This makes it possible to ensure that HE provision and learning outcomes are comparable and consistent at a threshold level across the UK. The purpose of the Quality Code is

- to safeguard the academic standards of UK HE;
- assure the academic quality of learning opportunities that UK HE offers;
- promote continuous and systematic improvement in UK HE;
- ensure that information about UK HE is fit for purpose, accessible and trustworthy.

HE providers use the Quality Code to help them maintain the academic standards of programmes and awards, assure and enhance the quality of learning opportunities, and to provide information about their HE provision. Student representatives and students' unions can use the Quality Code in their discussions with their institutes. Reviewers use the Quality Code as a benchmark for judging whether a HE provider meets UK expectations for academic standards, the quality of learning opportunities, enhancement and information. Reviews also take account of students' views on the performance of their HE provider. The Quality Code is based on a number of key values:

- Every student is treated fairly and with dignity, courtesy and respect.
- Every student has the opportunity to contribute to the shaping of their learning experience.
- Every student is properly and actively informed at appropriate times of matters relevant to their programmes of study.
- All policies and processes relating to study and programmes are clearly explained and transparent.
- Strategic oversight of academic standards and academic quality is at the highest level of academic governance of the provider.

- All policies and processes are regularly and effectively monitored, reviewed and improved.
- Sufficient and appropriate external involvement exists for the maintenance of academic standards and the quality of learning opportunities.
- All staff is supported, enabling them in turn to support students' learning experiences.

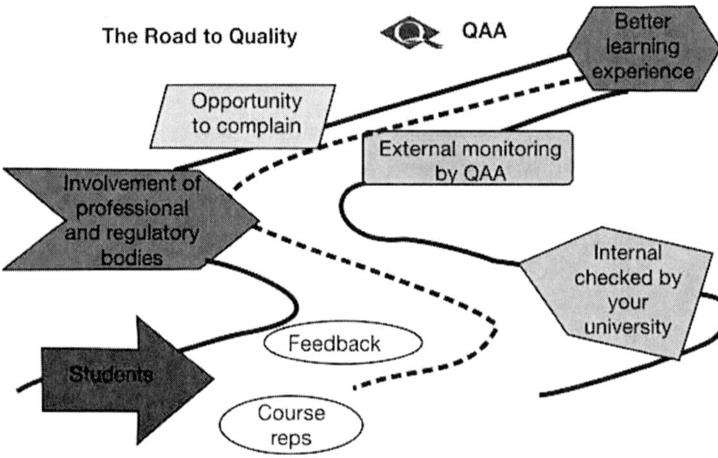

Figure 2.1: The Road to Quality—QAA

Expectations express key matters of principle that the HE sector has identified as essential for assuring academic standards and quality. They make clear what UK HE providers are required to do, what they expect of themselves and each other, and what students and the general public can therefore expect of providers. The Quality Code has been produced in consultation with the UK HE sector and is published and maintained by QAA on their behalf. QAA works with the sector to ensure that the Quality Code remains up to date, through an ongoing process of review and revision. The Quality Code relates to the learning and teaching activities of a higher education provider, including research degrees. Among the areas it does not cover are other forms of research activity, and estates management.

2.3 STANDARDS AND GUIDELINES FOR QUALITY ASSURANCE IN THE EUROPEAN HIGHER EDUCATION AREA (ESG)

A key goal of the Standards and Guidelines for Quality Assurance in the European Higher Education Area (ESG) is to contribute to the common understanding of quality assurance for learning and teaching across borders and among all stakeholders. They play an important role in the development of national and institutional quality assurance systems across the European Higher Education Area (EHEA) and cross-border cooperation. Engagement with quality assurance processes, particularly the external ones, allows European HE systems to demonstrate quality and increase transparency, thus helping to build mutual trust and better recognition of their qualifications, programmes and other provision.

The ESG are used by institutions and quality assurance agencies as a reference document for internal and external quality assurance systems in HE. Moreover, they are used by the European Quality Assurance Register (EQAR), which is responsible for the register of quality assurance agencies that comply with the ESG.

2.3.1 Scope and Concepts

The ESG are a set of standards and guidelines for internal and external quality assurance in higher education. The ESG provide guidance, covering the areas which are vital for successful quality provision and learning environments in HE. They include qualification frameworks, ECTS and diploma supplement that also contribute to promoting the transparency and mutual trust in HE in the EHEA. The focus of the ESG is on quality assurance related to learning and teaching in HE, including the learning environment and relevant links to research and innovation. In addition institutions have policies and processes to ensure and improve the quality of their other activities, such as research and governance.

The ESG have the following purposes:

- They set a common framework for quality assurance systems for learning and teaching at European, national and institutional level;
- They enable the assurance and improvement of quality of HE in the European HE area;
- They support mutual trust, thus facilitating recognition and mobility within and across national borders;
- They provide information on quality assurance in the EHEA.

2.3.2 Standards and Guidelines for Quality Assurance in the ESG

The Standards and Guidelines for Quality Assurance in the European Higher Education Area (ESG) were adopted in 2005 following a proposal prepared by the European Association for Quality Assurance in Higher Education (ENQA) in co-operation with the European Students' Union (ESU), the European Association of Institutions in Higher Education (EURASHE) and the European University Association (EUA). Since 2005, considerable progress has been made in quality assurance as well as in other Bologna action lines such as qualifications frameworks, recognition and the promotion of the use of learning outcomes, all these contributing to a paradigm shift towards student-centred learning and teaching. Given this changing context, in 2012 the Ministerial Communiqué invited the E4 Group (ENQA, ESU, EUA, and EURASHE) in cooperation with Education International (EI), BUSINESSEUROPE and the European Quality Assurance Register for Higher Education (EQAR) to prepare an initial proposal for a revised ESG "to improve their clarity, applicability and usefulness, including their scope".

The revision included several consultation rounds involving both the key stakeholder organizations and ministries. The many comments, proposals and recommendations received were carefully analyzed by the Steering Group (SG). They are reflected in this 2015 version of the ESG.

2.3.3 Recommendation by the Council

These purposes provide a framework within which the ESG may be used and implemented in different ways by different institutions, agencies and countries. The ESG provide the criteria at European level against which quality assurance agencies and their activities are assessed. This ensures that the quality assurance agencies in the EHEA adhere to the same set of principles and the processes and procedures are modelled to fit the purposes and requirements of their contexts. The ESG are based on the following four principles for quality assurance in the EHEA:

- HEIs have primary responsibility for the quality of their provision and its assurance;
- Quality assurance responds to the diversity of HE systems, institutions, programmes and students;
- Quality assurance supports the development of a quality culture;
- Quality assurance takes into account the needs and expectations of students, all other stakeholders and society.

The standards for quality assurance have been divided into three parts:

- Internal quality assurance
- External quality assurance
- Quality assurance agencies

The three parts are intrinsically interlinked and together form the basis for a European quality assurance framework. They work on a complementary basis in HEIs as well as in agencies and also work on the understanding that other stakeholders contribute to the framework. The guidelines explain why the standard is important and describe how standards might be implemented. They set out good practice in the relevant area for consideration by the actors involved in quality assurance. Implementation will vary depending on different contexts. Policies and processes are the main pillars of a coherent institutional quality assurance system that forms a cycle for continuous improvement and contributes to the accountability of the institution. It supports the development of quality culture in which all internal stakeholders assume responsibility for quality and engage in quality assurance at all levels of the institution. In order to facilitate this, the policy has a formal status and is publicly available.

In the new European HE is important to establish quality assurance systems that may be adapted to different national circumstances without forgetting the requirements in the European strategy. The strengths of universities reside increasingly in maintaining effective relationships with their environment, offering answers to the needs of all its stakeholders, placing them in the center of the academic and researcher processes.

The real value of the Quality Assurance System is its contribution to improving teaching, learning, research and public accountability. In other words, Systems Quality Assurance of the universities are structured demonstration of academic practice, which is described and is based on existing quality assurance and control processes of the different centers in the university. The objective of the System of Quality Assurance is the establishment of cyclic processes of planning, development, public information and feedback to promote the renewal and improvement of quality through self-reflexive criticism and based on objective data and actual results.

The quality manual lays the breakdown of procedures, highlighting the most relevant indicators of each procedure. The manual provides a solid basis on which the various centers design and build their own system of internal quality, facilitating the design and implementation of various procedures, evidence management, data collection and analysis of indicators and, finally, the standardization and systematization of improvement actions to ensure the quality of degrees, masters and doctorates teachings. The basic objectives and procedure manual is to ensure quality of all the degrees, reviewed and improved whenever deemed necessary to their training, based on the needs and expectations of different stakeholders to which they will promptly inform and keep updated about the Quality Assurance System.

The Quality Assurance System indicates guidelines related to:

- New programme design—whether the programmes are designed with overall objectives, intended learning outcomes, student-centred learning, stimulating students' motivation, self-reflection and engagement in the learning process.
- Providing conditions and support that are necessary for students to make progress in their academic career in the best interest of the individual students, programmes, institutions and systems.
- Physical resources such as libraries, study facilities and IT infrastructure to human support in the form of tutors, counsellors and other advisers.
- The internal quality assurance ensures that all resources are fit for purpose, accessible, and that students are informed about the services available to them.
- Effective processes to collect and analyze information about study programmes and other activities feed into the internal quality assurance system.
- Institutions provide information about their activities, including the programmes they offer and the selection criteria for them, the intended learning outcomes of these programmes, the qualifications they award, the teaching, learning and assessment procedures used, the pass rates and the learning opportunities available to their students as well as graduate employment information.
- Regular monitoring, review and revision of study programmes aim to ensure that the provision remains appropriate and to create a supportive and effective learning environment for students.

- External quality assurance in its various forms can verify the effectiveness of institutions' internal quality assurance, act as a catalyst for improvement and offer the institution new perspectives.
- There is link between internal and external quality assurance. These may be addressed differently, depending on the type of external quality assurance.
- At the core of external quality assurance is the wide range of expertise provided by peer experts, who contribute to the work of the agency through input from various perspectives, including those of institutions, academics, students and employers/ professional practitioners.
- The report by the experts is the basis for the institution's follow-up action of the external evaluation and it provides information to society regarding the activities of an institution.
- In an appeal's procedure, the institution questions the formal outcomes of the process, where it can demonstrate that the outcome is not based on sound evidence, that criteria have not been correctly applied or that the processes have not been consistently implemented.
- The goals and objectives of the quality assurance activities are described and published along with the nature of interaction between the agencies and relevant stakeholders in HE, especially the HEIs, and the scope of the agencies' work. The expertise in the agency may be increased by including international members in agency committees.
- A variety of external quality assurance activities are carried out by agencies to achieve different objectives. Among them is evaluation, review, audit, assessment, accreditation or other similar activities at programme or institutional level that may be carried out differently.
- A periodic external review helps the agency to reflect on its policies and activities. It provides a means

for assuring the agency and its stakeholders that it continues to adhere to the principles enshrined in the ESG.

2.4 QUALITY ASSURANCE IN US EDUCATION SYSTEM

The American HE sector is diverse and creative. A leader in innovation for decades, it produces cutting edge research and contributes mightily to the American economy. United States spends a larger percentage of GDP on HE than any other country. Quality assurance procedures have several forms in the U.S. education system. The approval of institutions and programs is generally undertaken by state agencies and accrediting agencies, with the accrediting agencies are responsible for the establishment and maintenance of academic and administrative standards too. Professional and academic disciplinary associations also play a role in influencing and assessing quality. Educational potential, progress, and outcomes, as well as inputs and outputs, are measured by surveys, studies, tests, and other assessments at the national, regional, state and institutional levels.

There are more than 7,000 institutions of higher education in the United States. The sector is diverse, with everything from large public research institutions to small religious colleges to for-profit institutions located fully on the web, and much in between. Recognizing this diversity, government has historically taken a flexible approach to the regulation of HE. States prescribe methods and processes by which institutions operate, but in general, HEIs have been given the flexibility to set their own goals and determine the methods by which they will achieve them. Key characteristics of US HE are:

- Autonomy
- Self-regulation
- Diversity
- Integration
- Diversified financing
- Trust

The Higher Education Act (HEA) of 1965 created the federal system of HE finance. But it does not state teaching, research, or service to the community. It states that an institution must be "accredited" for its students to be eligible for grants and student loans. Accreditation is a non-governmental system under which regional or national private entities work with individual HEIs to review and critique their operations. The HEI provides a "self-assessment" that the accreditor then uses as a framework for examining the institution's successes and challenges.

Accreditation has been around for more than a century. Before World War II, accreditation was a fully non-governmental initiative that provided a process for institutions to assess themselves, and it also served as a basis upon which institutions would allow students to transfer from one to another. Since the 1950s, non-governmental accreditors help the federal government by certifying that institutions are worthy of participation in HE financial programs. The Institutional Accreditation Process consists of the following:

- Self-study (18-24 months)
- What are we doing?
- How good are our results? (How do we know?)
- What should we be doing differently?
- Peer evaluation
- Commission's decision on accreditation

The basis of accreditation are whether

- The institution has goals and activities appropriate for HE
- The institution has the resources necessary to achieve those goals
- The institution is achieving those goals
- The institution has the capacity to continue achieving those goals

The initial accreditation process for a new institution is especially detailed and can take between five and ten years to complete. After initial accreditation, for most institutions, re-accreditation happens every ten years, providing an opportunity for them to update their goals and methods evaluate themselves. The regulation of HE is flexible. Institutions set their own goals and measures that indicate progress toward them. Academic priorities are established internally, and institutions themselves assess whether they are successfully pursuing them. The flexibility of the accreditation system allows it to be responsive to the diversity of HE. If an accreditor finds that the organization has not met the basic requirements of financial stability and academic rigor, the institution is no longer eligible to participate in federal financial aid programs.

To enhance the strength of the regulatory system, HEA was amended in 1992 to require the U.S. Department of Education (ED) to approve accreditors. The ED must certify that each accrediting agency has the capacity to assess HEIs. The amended HEA gave more direction to accreditors, requiring them to certify that institutions meet "minimum standards" in ten areas, including student achievement. Some institutions began to create voluntary accountability and quality assurance frameworks based largely on outcomes, regarding finance, student outcomes, campus life and experiences, employment, graduation and retention and other information relevant to applicant decision-making.

Many states have adopted "outcomes-based funding" or "performance-based funding" (PBF), which identify particular outcome targets and "rewards" institutions for meeting these targets. The gainful employment policy proposed did not work. While regional accreditors don't use statistical outcome measures or minimum standards for accreditation, most national and programmatic accreditors set threshold requirements like completion rates, exam pass rates, and employment rates. Many institutions argued that the use of a common framework would lead to homogenization and increase the burden of compliance.

The rating systems reveal outcome-related transparency and accountability, as well as challenges inherent in performance-based regulation. Even if there is a general consensus on aspirations like accessibility, affordability, and quality, defining those goals concretely, measuring them meaningfully, and then applying them uniformly to the highly heterogeneous sector has its own problems. Institutions seek to gain outcome metrics, while failing to advance the underlying goals not counted like equitable access to HE. It raises high competition amongst institutes.

Some of the organizations associated with US HE are:

- American Association of Collegiate Registrars and Admissions Officers (AACRAO) is a national organization providing extensive resources and information on the technical and managerial aspects of academic decision-making at all levels.
- Association for Institutional Research (AIR) is a national association of professional analysts, located at academic institutions, who conduct research to advise their institutions on quality issues including admissions, facilities, staffing, management, and costs, among others, and who also conduct comparative and benchmarking studies.
- Council for the Advancement and Support of Education (CASE) is an organization promoting the principles and practice of fund-raising, public relations, and alumni relations, all of which are important to building and maintaining quality in autonomous HEIs.
- Society for College and University Planning (SCUP) is an academic strategic planning organization that provides information and resources on the practice of planning and assessing institutional academics, facilities, finances, strategies and other services.
- Center for Quality Assurance in International Education (CQAIE) is a US-based organization providing information and resources on quality assurance, globalization, and standard-setting.
- International Network of Quality Assurance Agencies in Higher Education (INQAAHE) is a global organization of national quality assurance

and accreditation authorities dedicated to improving practices and information-sharing. Several recognized US accrediting agencies plus the Council for Higher Education Accreditation (CHEA) are members of INQAAHE.

- UNESCO Higher Education Quality Assurance and Recognition Activity provides information and resources on UNESCO initiatives in quality assurance, including the global network of recognition information agreements and capacity-building projects.

2.5 QUALITY ASSURANCE IN AUSTRALIAN HIGHER EDUCATION

The Tertiary Education Quality and Standards Agency (TEQSA) is Australia's independent national regulator of the HE sector. TEQSA is the agency for providers or registered providers of HE courses. The Australian Skills Quality Authority (ASQA) is the national regulator for the vocational education and training sector and registered training organisations. Both ASQA and TEQSA have powers to register providers to deliver courses to overseas students, as well as to investigate and instigate enforcement action against registered providers for breaches of the National Code. ASQA and TEQSA also have oversight responsibilities for English Language Intensive Courses for Overseas Students (ELICOS) and foundation programs, except where these courses are delivered in the capacity of a school.

The AQF (Australian Quality Framework) puts senior secondary school, vocational education and training (VET) and HE qualifications into a single, national framework. It has played an important role in the quality assurance of Australia's well-regarded tertiary education system and sets out the nature and purpose of senior secondary education. The AQF is used to assist recognition of Australian qualifications in other countries and has served as a model for the development of qualifications frameworks internationally. The AQF has 10 levels that include descriptions of learning outcomes in terms of knowledge, skills and their application at increasing levels of complexity.

In Australia, a number of factors figured in the development of the AQF. Reforms to adopt competency-based training, prompting a need for nationally recognised qualifications linked to competency standards. This highlighted a need for greater consistency and transparency between qualifications to support recognition of prior learning (RPL) and credit transfer. In its initial form, the AQF was a relatively loose framework. The 2008 Review of Higher Education (Bradley Review) proposed that Australia should develop a more coherent tertiary education system. It noted the need for a continuum of tertiary skills and recommended a single regulator and funding source for higher education sectors The Review of the AQF took place between 2009 and 2011 under the authority of the AQF Council, which was established as a result of stakeholders wanting "a stronger custodian of a stronger AQF". In 2011, a revised AQF was implemented with features, including a more consistent taxonomy of learning outcomes. The taxonomy was applied to both levels and qualifications, making the AQF a more detailed and complex document.

Major contextual issues for the review were skills and knowledge which are increasingly important, qualifications, as well as experience help to get jobs, employers may use qualifications to select between job seekers, nature of work is changing, recognise new skills and learning methods. As the AQF is a framework for qualification types, social and enterprise skills should be able to be related to the core content of the qualification, acquired through the process of learning and teaching, assessed and reported in ways that are fair, valid and reliable. Some enterprise and social skills are included in the AQF.

The AQF currently sets out certain non-discipline specific generic skills that students can acquire through learning that include some enterprise and social skills. They are fundamental skills (literacy, numeracy), people skills (working with others, communication), thinking skills (learning to learn, decision making, problem solving) and personal skills (self-direction, acting with integrity). The AQF states that application of these generic skills is specific to the education or training sector. The AQF variably incorporates its generic skills in the level and qualification descriptors. The descriptors refer to communication, some form of problem solving and autonomy. Only the learning outcomes for the senior secondary certificate of education include fundamental skills such as literacy and numeracy. While school should provide a foundation of literacy and numeracy, tertiary education may be expected to expand these skills. When the AQF Council was disbanded in 2014, the Commonwealth Minister for Education agreed the AQF would be reviewed within five years.

The 2017-18 Commonwealth Budget included a measure for the Higher Education Standards Panel (HESP) to oversee a review of the Higher Education Provider Category Standards (PCS). The PCS describe different categories of HE providers, and requirements expected of them, for registration by the Tertiary Education Quality and Standards Agency (TEQSA). The PCS are part of the *Higher Education Standards Framework (Threshold Standards) 2015* which sets the high standards required to operate as a 'HE provider' or 'university' in Australia. The PCS fulfil a range of functions.

Australia is positioned well by a strong and dynamic HE system. The PCS, as part of the Threshold Standards, have helped set requirements for the quality HE system that exists today. Australia could continue to operate under the existing PCS. However, the sector is not static and nor therefore should be its PCS. It is important that Australia consider how it wants the PCS to support a quality HE sector for the future. This review provides an opportunity to reflect on the current usage of the PCS and pivot, if required, to best capitalise on the strengths of an evolving sector. As such, this is an opportunity to consider the PCS through a contemporary and critical lens, to ensure they are fit for purpose against Australia's changing HE landscape, comparable to international benchmarks, and accommodating to innovative and changing practice.

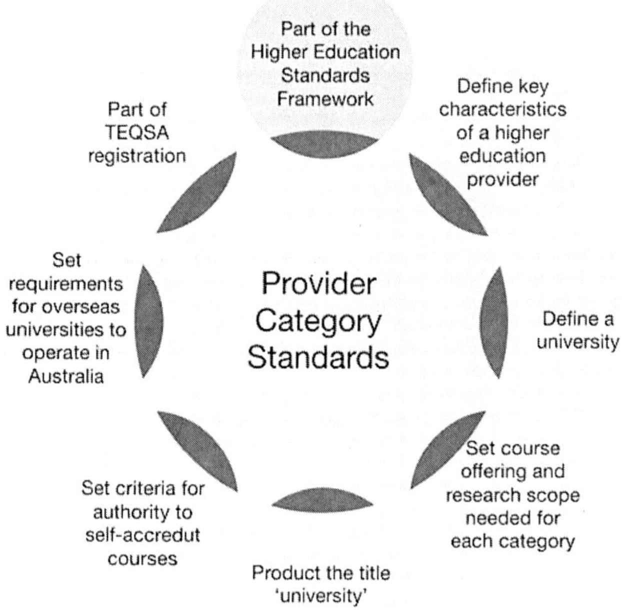

Figure 2.2: Provider Category Standards in Australian HE

The PCS are part of Australia's national quality assurance framework and are set out in Part B: Criteria for Higher Education Providers of the Threshold Standards. They classify the types of education providers that can be registered by the national HE regulator TEQSA to deliver HE in Australia. The PCS reflect and formalise key elements of differentiation in Australia's HE sector, particularly the distinctions between providers that may label themselves as a 'University' or non-university 'HE Provider'. All providers of HE that gain registration by TEQSA through meeting the Threshold Standards become a 'HE Provider'. This title signals to the public that they are a provider of quality HE in Australia. Those that meet additional criteria in research, scholarship and community engagement may seek approval from TEQSA to be registered in one of the university categories.

The National Code 2018 sets standards to ensure education services meet the needs and expectations of overseas students who come to Australia, and satisfy the objectives of the Education Services for Overseas Students Act (ESOS Act). The National Code complements the strong quality assurance frameworks used by government agencies to oversee the Australian education system. ESOS agencies may use information given by providers for other purposes in assessing their registration or compliance under the ESOS Act. The National Code has legal effect as expressly provided for by the ESOS Act. Therefore, breaches of the National Code by registered providers can result in actions being taken against a registered provider, including suspension or cancellation of registration. The ESOS legislative framework is administered by a number of agencies across the Commonwealth and states and territories.

2.6 INDIAN HIGHER EDUCATION ACCREDITATION SYSTEM

India has one of the largest and diverse education systems in the world. Privatization, widespread expansion, increased autonomy and introduction of programmes in new and emerging areas have improved access to HE. At the same time, it has also led to widespread concern on the quality and relevance of the HE. To address these concerns, the National Policy on Education (NPE, 1986) and the Programme of Action (PoA, 1992) spelt out strategic plans for the policies, advocated the establishment of an independent national accreditation agency. Consequently, the National Assessment and Accreditation Council (NAAC) were established in 1994 as an autonomous institution of the University Grants Commission (UGC). The mandate of NAAC as reflected in its vision statement is in making quality assurance an integral part of the functioning of HEIs. Distance education and offshore campuses are not covered by NAAC.

NAAC promotes self and external quality evaluation and sustenance initiatives. NAAC's engagement and endeavor as given below:

- To arrange for periodic assessment and accreditation of institutions of HE or units thereof, or specific academic programmes or projects,
- To stimulate the academic environment for promotion of quality in teaching-learning and research in HEIs,
- To encourage self-evaluation, accountability, autonomy and innovations in HE,
- To undertake quality-related research studies, consultancy and training programmes, and
- To collaborate with other stakeholders of higher education for quality evaluation, promotion and sustenance.

The National Assessment and Accreditation Council (NAAC) has brought revised process from July 2017. The main focus of the revision has been to enhance the redeeming features of the accreditation process and make them more robust, objective, transparent and scalable as well as ICT enabled and reduced duration of accreditation process. NAAC primarily focuses on assessment of the quality of HEIs in the country. The NAAC methodology for Assessment and Accreditation consists of self-assessment by the institution along with external peer assessment organized by NAAC.

2.6.1 Core Values

The accreditation framework of NAAC is based on five core values detailed below:

- Contributing to National Development
- Fostering Global Competencies among Students
- Inculcating a Value System among Students
- Promoting the Use of Technology

2.6.2 Assessment and Accreditation of Higher Education Institutions

The NAAC has been carrying out the process of quality assessment and accreditation of HEIs over the past two decades. Several HEIs have gone through this process and a sizeable number has also undergone subsequent cycles of accreditation.

Over years the feedback procured from the HEIs, other stakeholders and the developments in the national scene all have contributed in making appropriate revisions in the process so as to accelerate the process with greater quality rigor. The Revised Assessment and Accreditation Framework were launched in July 2017. It represents an explicit paradigm shift making it ICT enabled, objective, transparent, scalable and robust. The shift is

- from qualitative peer judgement to data-based quantitative indicator evaluation with increased objectivity and transparency
- towards extensive use of ICT confirming scalability and robustness
- in terms of simplification of the process drastic reduction in number of questions, size of the report, visit days, and so on
- in terms of boosting benchmarking as quality improvement tool. This has been attempted through comparison of NAAC indicators with other international QA frameworks
- introducing pre-qualifier for peer team visit, as 30% of system generated score
- introducing System Generated Scores (SGS) with combination of online evaluation (about 70%) and peer judgement (about 30%)
- introducing the element of third party validation of data
- in providing appropriate differences in the metrics, weightages and benchmarks to universities, autonomous colleges and affiliated/constituent colleges
- in revising several metrics to bring in enhanced participation of students and alumni in the assessment process.

2.6.3 Quality Indicator Framework (QIF)—Description

The criteria-based assessment forms the backbone of A&A process of NAAC. The seven criteria represent the core functions and activities of a HEI. In the revised framework not only the academic and administrative aspects of institutional functioning but also the emerging issues have been included. The seven criteria to serve as basis for assessment of HEIs are:

- Curricular Aspects
- Teaching-learning and Evaluation
- Research, Innovations and Extension
- Infrastructure and Learning Resources
- Student Support and Progression
- Governance, Leadership and Management
- Institutional Values and Best Practices

Under each criterion a few key indicators are identified. These key indicators (KIs) are further delineated as metrics which actually elicit responses from the HEIs. These seven criteria along with their KIs are given below explicating the aspects they represent.

Criterion 1 pertains to the practices of an institution in initiating a wide range of programme options and courses that are in tune with the emerging national and global trends and relevant to the local needs. Apart from issues of diversity and academic flexibility, aspects on career orientation, multi-skill development, feedback system and involvement of stakeholders in curriculum updating are also gauged. Key indicators:

1.1 Curriculum Design and Development

1.2 Curriculum Planning and Implementation

1.3 Academic Flexibility

1.4 Curriculum Enrichment

1.5 Feedback System

Criterion 2 pertains to the efforts of an institution to serve students of different backgrounds and abilities, through effective teaching-learning experiences. Interactive instructional techniques that engage students in higher order 'thinking' and investigation, through the use of interviews, focused group discussions, debates, projects, presentations, experiments, practicum, internship and application of ICT resources are important considerations. It also probes into the adequacy, competence as well as the continuous professional development of the faculty who handle the programmes of study. The efficiency of the techniques used to continuously evaluate the performance of teachers and students is also a major concern of this criterion. Key indicators:

2.1 Student Enrolment and Profile
2.2 Catering to Student Diversity
2.3 Teaching-learning Process
2.4 Teacher Profile and Quality
2.5 Evaluation Process and Reforms
2.6 Student Performance and Learning Outcomes
2.7 Student Satisfaction Survey

Criterion 3—Research, Innovations and Extension

This criterion seeks information on the policies, practices and outcomes of the institution, with reference to research, innovations and extension. It deals with the facilities provided and efforts made by the institution to promote a 'research culture'. The institution has the responsibility to enable faculty to undertake research projects useful to the society. Serving the community through extension, which is a social responsibility and a core value to be demonstrated by institutions, is also a major aspect of this criterion. Key indicators:

3.1 Promotion of Research and Facilities
3.2 Resource Mobilization for Research
3.3 Innovation Ecosystem
3.4 Research Publications and Awards
3.5 Consultancy
3.6 Extension Activities
3.7 Collaboration

Criterion 4—Infrastructure and Learning Resources

The adequacy and optimal use of the facilities available in an institution are essential to maintain the quality of academic and other programmes on the campus. It also requires information on how every constituent of the institution—students, teachers and staff—benefits from these facilities. Expansion of facilities to meet future development is included among other concerns. Key indicators:

4.1 Physical Facilities

4.2 Library as a Learning Resource

4.3 IT Infrastructure

4.4 Maintenance of Campus Infrastructure

Criterion 5—Student Support and Progression

The highlights of this criterion are the efforts of an institution to provide necessary assistance to students, to enable them to acquire meaningful experiences for learning at the campus and to facilitate their holistic development and progression. It also looks into student performance and alumni profiles and the progression of students to HE and gainful employment. Key indicators:

5.1 Student Support

5.2 Student Progression

5.3 Student Participation and Activities

5.4 Alumni Engagement

Criterion 6—Governance, Leadership and Management

Effective functioning of an institution can be gauged by the policies and practices it has evolved in the matter of planning human resources, recruitment, training, performance appraisal, financial management and the overall role of leadership. Key indicators:

6.1 Institutional Vision and Leadership

6.2 Strategy Development and Deployment

6.3 Faculty Empowerment Strategies

6.4 Financial Management and Resource Mobilization

6.5 Internal Quality Assurance System (IQAS)

Criterion 7—Institutional Values and Best Practices

An educational institution operates in the context of the larger education system in the country. In order to be relevant in changing national and global contexts an educational institution has to be responsive to the emerging challenges and pressing issues. It has a social responsibility to be proactive in the efforts towards development in the larger contexts. This role of the institution is reflected in terms of the kinds of programmes, activities and preferences (values) that it incorporates within its regular functioning. The extent to which an institution is impactful in this is a sure reflection of its quality.

Every institution has a mandate to be responsive to at least a few pressing issues such as gender equity, environmental consciousness and sustainability, inclusiveness and professional ethics, but the way it addresses these and evolves practices will always be unique. Practices which are evolved internally by the institution leading to improvements in any one aspect of its functioning—academic, administrative or organizational, are recognized as a "best practices". Over a period of time, due to such unique ways of functioning each institution develops distinct characteristic which becomes its recognizable attribute. Key indicators:

7.1 Institutional Values and Social Responsibilities

7.2 Best Practices

7.3 Institutional Distinctiveness

2.6.4 The Assessment Process

Taking cognizance of the diversity in the kinds of institutions HEIs have been grouped under three categories, namely universities, autonomous colleges and affiliated/constituent colleges.

The assessment process is carried out in three stages. As stated earlier, it will comprise three main components, viz. Self Study Report (SSR), Student Satisfaction Survey and the Peer Team Report. The SSR has a total of 137 metrics for universities covering the seven criteria described earlier. The SSR has two kinds of metrics—quantitative and qualitative metrics.

2.6.5 Assessment Outcome

The final result of the assessment and accreditation exercise will be an ICT-based score, which is a combination of evaluation of qualitative and quantitative metrics. This will be compiled as a document comprising three parts.

Part I is Peer Team Report. Section 1 gives the general information of the institution. Section 2 gives criterion-wise analysis based on peer evaluation of qualitative indicators, which is qualitative, descriptive assessment based on critical analysis, strengths and weaknesses. Section 3 presents an overall analysis which includes SWOC analysis. Section 4 are recommendations for quality enhancement. Part II is graphical representation based on Quantitative Metrics (QnM). This is a System Generated Quality Profile based on statistical analysis of quantitative indicators in the NAAC's QIF (quality indicator framework). Graphical presentation of institutional features would be reflected through synthesis of quantifiable indicators. Part III is Institutional Grade Sheet. This contains the Institutional Grade Sheet which is based on qualitative indicators, quantitative indicators and student satisfaction survey using existing calculation methods but it will be generated by a software. The above three parts put together form "NAAC Accreditation Outcome" document. It is mandatory to display it on their institutional website apart from NAAC hosting it on its website.

2.6.6 Calculation of Institutional CGPA

The CGPA is calculated based on the scores obtained from the three sources, viz. the System Generated Scores (SGS) of the QnM which comprise about 70% of the total, the scores from the qualitative metrics includes critical appraisal by the peer team through on site visit and the scores obtained on the Student Satisfaction Survey. These will be collated through an automated procedure based on 'benchmarks' and assessed on a five points scale, viz. (0, 1, 2, 3 and 4).

2.6.7 The Final Grade

On the basis of the CGPA obtained by the institution in maximum possible score of 4.00, the final grade is assigned on a seven points scale as shown in Table 2.1. The seven point refers to the seven letter grades each aligned to the seven specific score range.

Table 2.1: Indian Higher Education Accreditation System—Final Grades

Range of Institutional Cumulative Grade Point Average (CGPA)	Letter Grade	Status
3.51-4.00	A++	Accredited
3.26-3.50	A+	Accredited
3.01-3.25	A	Accredited
2.76-3.00	B++	Accredited
2.51-2.75	B+	Accredited
2.01-2.50	B	Accredited
1.51-2.00	C	Accredited
≤ 1.50	D	Not Accredited

Institutions which secure a CGPA equal to or less than 1.50 are notionally categorized under the letter grade "D". Such unqualified institutions will also be intimated and notified by NAAC as "Assessed and Found not Qualified for Accreditation". To provide a review mechanism for institutions who are aggrieved about the process or its outcome or any other issues related thereof, the NAAC has evolved Mechanism for Institutional Appeals. Institutions which would like to make an improvement in the accredited status, can volunteer for re-assessment, after completing at least one year, but not after the completion of three years. The option can be exercised only once in a cycle. Re-assessed institution cannot come for another re-assessment in the same cycle. Due consideration is given to the post-accreditation activities resulting in quality improvement, quality sustenance and quality enhancement.

3

Designing a Programme and Inducting Students

3.1 PROGRAMME DESIGN

Designing a programme is a creative activity and encourages innovation. It is an iterative process of development and is based on feedback from a range of sources, including other staff, students, employers and professional, statutory and regulatory bodies. It is the responsibility of the education institutions to ensure academic standards and quality, while ensuring a process of continuous improvement. The institutions decide what programmes to offer within the context of their organizational mission and other strategic factors. These may include government policies, economic growth and to support strategically important and vulnerable subjects, an assessment of student demand for existing and new programmes, and advice from external bodies such as employers and industry about workforce needs. This enables institutions to offer a variety of programmes reflecting the needs of an increasingly diverse range of students.

Various persons and departments are involved in programme development where the responsibilities are clearly defined and understood, and all those involved are made aware of the outcomes of decisions. It is also included in the strategic and academic resources planning, within the context. It helps in assessing whether sufficient and appropriate physical, human and learning resources are available for a new programme. The approval depends on evidence from analysis of viability and academic merits, where efficiency may be improved or duplication reduced by aligning requirements with requirements of professional, statutory and regulatory bodies.

According to the UK Quality Code, when developing a programme, it is considered that the purpose of the programme is within the context of the strategic approach; knowledge, understanding and skills intended for intake; personal, professional, academic development; research; employment; structure and components of the programme; learning outcomes and learning and teaching activities. How students are enabled to achieve outcomes; workload, progression and increasing intellectual demand, with sufficient flexibility for special requirements; balance between practical and academic load; modes of study; the use of technology; direct and self-study hours; subject content; programme is coherent, in terms of its logic, structure and intellectual integrity; evaluation mechanisms.

3.1.1 Processes for Designing a Programme

The processes of programme design and development are an essential part of internal quality assurance. The processes are transparent and an appropriate level of resource is applied to ensure the outcomes. Processes include data collection through market research, student performance measures and feedback, and other organisational information; identify any differential impact on particular groups of students; approval of records for future reference, including name for the programme, period of delivery, subject to monitoring and review; responsibility for managing the process, timescales, and the criteria on which decisions are taken; responsibility and mechanisms for identifying, disseminating and embedding good practices; regular evaluation of processes for organisational improvement determines how often they carry out such evaluation relating to outcomes and enhancement of learning; existing programmes which undergo substantial change; processes for managing minor changes to programmes and closure of an existing programme.

3.1.2 External Expertise

Taking advice from persons external to the systems helps in maintaining academic standards and quality. Educators involved in teaching different subjects or from professional services or from other organisations, depending on their role, will bring independence and objectivity to the decisions taken leading to transparency and compares academic standards across. Externals provide additional perspectives and expertise on current developments in the subject area and in learning and teaching practices. The nature and extent of external input is proportionate to the stage of the process. Students will make a valuable contribution with their own experience and that of others. Student participation may be formal or informal, and at different levels. The roles and responsibilities are clear. Feedback and contribution of all students involved is ensured by appropriate training and support.

Staff from across and from other organisations, academic teaching staff, professional services staff, such as educational developers and learning technologists, employers will help. Appropriate support, training and continuing personal and professional development helps in efficiency. Facilitate staff to work together, so that they are able to draw on their collective experience and develop innovative ideas. Facilitate staff that have not been part of the process but are involved in teaching or supporting student learning to gain an understanding of the aims, structure and content of the programme. Recognise the value and facilitate staff involvement in programme design and development at other institutions.

3.2 INDUCTING STUDENTS

According to UK Quality Code, transparency in providing information to students and involving students at various levels like delivery of courses, evaluation, curriculum development and governance can work if they are equipped adequately with the required tools to carry out the activities in an effective manner and help in quality education standards. Information is structured to communicate the purposes and value of higher education to the public at large, to help prospective students make informed decisions about where, what, when and how they will study, to enable current students to make the most of their higher education learning opportunities, to confirm the achievements of students on completion of their studies, to safeguard academic standards and assure and enhance academic quality.

The concern should not be with the mechanisms used to produce information, nor the media chosen to communicate it, but with the quality of the information in terms of whether it is fit for purpose, accessible and trustworthy. HEIs target the intended stakeholders, who use information for their own specific purposes and set their own priorities concerning where to seek, how to choose and use, and when to look for the information they require. The United Kingdom and Scotland have a Quality Code which clearly defines the expectations for information sharing from educational institutions which are given below, and as defined by the Quality Assurance Agency (QAA).

Some of this information is of direct interest to the public at large and should be accessible to and retrievable by everyone. Other information may be of a more specialist, detailed nature and relevant to more limited audiences, such as prospective or current students or those who have completed their studies. Further assurance to the public can be provided when the University Grants Commission (UGC) and National Accreditation & Assessment Council (NAAC) reports on its scrutiny of the way education institutions conduct themselves and use internal information, which is not normally in the public domain, to safeguard academic standards and to assure and enhance academic quality.

3.2.1 Information for Public

Education institutions should provide information for the public about the learning opportunities they offer that is fit for purpose, accessible and trustworthy. Information that HEIs produce should be timely, current, transparent, and focused on the needs of the stakeholders. Information should be available and easily retrievable, taking into account the diversity. Education institutions should publish information that describes their mission, values and overall strategy. Information is published about organisational structure, the composition of the student population, the different modes of study that are supported, and the programmes and qualifications offered. Information may include governance arrangements, corporate and strategic plans, and annual reports.

The information enables stakeholders and users to develop an understanding of its profile. Publish policies concerning information and data. Information is published in formats that suit both the institutes and the stakeholders' needs and purposes.

3.2.2 Information for Prospective Students

It covers those who are exploring the possibility of studying with a particular education institution, from showing an initial interest, through the applications and admissions process, till they register, as indicated by the QAA. Not only prospective students but also their parents, advisers, sponsors or supporters require access to information about the education institution and its processes. Some of the information that is relevant for the public at large will also be of interest to prospective students. More detailed information is necessary to help prospective students make informed decisions about the location of study; the programme of study and qualification; the mode of study; and the support they will need. Information is published for all categories of prospective students, international students, undergraduates and postgraduates. Prospective students may also wish to access information that is primarily targeted at current students.

They should be directed to the relevant application, selection, admission and registration/enrolment process, and other relevant sources of information. Entry requirements are specified along with details of other required prior experience where appropriate. The processes for the recognition of prior learning for the purpose of meeting entry requirements or for other non-standard entry considerations are described. Costs of study, including full details of fees, additional costs associated, and any scholarships that may be available. Necessary information pertaining to academic environment to enable their development and achievement, nature and design of the curriculum provides an overview of likely opportunities, learning and assessment methods; and of the resources and facilities available. Inclusive learning environment is provided for students to ensure equality of opportunity, and how they anticipate and respond to the diverse needs of students. Indicative information about teaching, research and supervisors; learning and teaching spaces; libraries; learning environments such as laboratories and studios; communication and information technologies, virtual learning environments, etc.

Connections with industry, business and the professions, including links with professional, statutory and regulatory bodies and employers, accreditation status helps. Study abroad and other international learning experiences, how well their programme is performing, including employment and further study; satisfaction levels. Other services, student participation, student representative body where applicable, accommodation and social and recreation facilities, study modes and options, etc.

3.2.3 Information for Current Students

The information provided to prospective students is useful for current. They need information at a greater level of detail in order to make the most of their higher education experience. Education institutes should therefore ensure that all such information is up to date and brought to the attention of current students at the appropriate time. Information on the programme of study is issued to current students at the start of their programme and throughout their studies. Programme-level guides or handbooks—electronic or hard copy. Information may be provided about learning outcomes at programme and module level curriculum details, including options to be selected, scheduled learning and teaching activities; guided independent study; study abroad; the structural and administrative arrangements, supervision arrangements, assessment details, including content, timing, deadlines for submission, marking criteria, and giving feedback. Details about alumni services, career advice, and further study should be provided.

Responsibilities of students, and what they are entitled to expect from their education institution, inclusive learning experience, equality of opportunity, diverse needs of students, facilities provided to support learning, placements, international learning experiences, and any other opportunities associated with the programme. Set out how they engage with students, feedback, regulations and procedures for the interruption of study, good academic practices, academic appeals and student complaints, student conduct, and professional conduct, etc.

3.2.4 Information for Students on Completion of their Studies

Current students become alumni after leaving on the completion of their studies. The relationship between education institution and their students may extend beyond this point. When students leave their programme of study, education institutes issue to them a detailed record of their studies, which gives evidence to others of the students' achievement in their academic programme. Education institutes should have rigorous mechanisms in place to safeguard the integrity of records of students' academic achievements. Detailed records of study are produced not only for students who complete their programme of study but also for those who exit the programme before completion.

Students are provided with a record of their academic achievement within a reasonable time of completion or termination of their studies. Education institutes specify the length of time for which they will archive records of student achievements and communicate clearly their policies for archiving and retrieving such records. Procedures for the issue of replacement records are subject to appropriate checks on the validity of the request. Where institutes choose to make available information on their students' non-academic achievements, they ensure that these are a fair and accurate reflection of those achievements.

3.2.5 Information for Regulatory Bodies

Education institutes produce information to enable those with responsibility for setting and maintaining academic standards and assuring and enhancing academic quality, both internally and externally, to discharge their duties effectively. This information, which is not necessarily in the public domain and may be commercially sensitive, is, nevertheless, subject to scrutiny through periodic external reviews.

Education institutes set out their framework for managing academic standards and quality assurance and enhancement and describe the data and information used to support its implementation maintain records of all arrangements for delivering higher education with others that are subject to a formal agreement. Education institutes ensure that information about their arrangements for the management of academic standards, quality assurance and enhancement is transparently and consistently documented and that all those with responsibility for academic standards and quality, internally and externally, are fully informed about what is expected of them. This information may take the form of a code of practice, quality handbook, strategy, or equivalent, produced in hard or electronic copy.

This information is supplemented by categories of data and management information determined and used by the institute in implementing processes and procedures for the management of academic standards and quality. Where learning opportunities are delivered with others, responsibility for academic standards and quality rests with the university which awards degree, which documents clearly the procedures that it has developed to assure itself that the delegation of operational aspects of the management of standards and quality to the partner, delivery organisation or support provider is effective. This information specifies the respective roles and responsibilities of the university awarding degrees, partners, delivery organisations and support providers in relation to the management of academic standards and the quality of learning opportunities.

These may include promotion and publicity, recruitment, selection and admission, learning, teaching and assessment, management of student records, and quality assurance, as mentioned in the UK Quality Code. Data and management information are used to promote effective management of academic standards and quality across the organisation. Educational institutes determine the precise nature of this information according to their prevailing management style and culture. The UGC should set out the expectation concerning public information which education institutions are required to meet.

3.2.6 Information for Stakeholders

The educational institutions should produce information for their intended stakeholders about the learning opportunities they offer that is fit for purpose, accessible and trustworthy, as stressed upon by the QAA UK as given below:

- Publish information that describes mission, values and overall strategy.
- Describe the process for application and admission to the programme of study.
- Publish information to help prospective students select their programme with an understanding of the academic environment in which they will be studying and the provision that will be made to enable their development and achievement.
- Information on the programme of study is issued to current students at the start of their programme and throughout their studies.
- Set out what they expect of current students and what current students can expect of the education institution.
- When students leave their programme of study, issue to them a detailed record of their studies, which gives evidence to others of the students' achievement in their academic programme.
- Set out their arrangements for managing academic standards and quality assurance and enhancement and describe the data and information used to support its implementation maintain records of all arrangements for delivering higher education with others that are subject to a formal agreement.

4
Teaching and Lifelong Learning

4.1 TEACHING LEARNING

Institutions provide learning opportunities through short-term/long-term programmes, including wide variety of modes of both learning and teaching, in different combinations. Identifying effective learning and teaching is complex, as it is influenced by many factors, which vary between individuals and different learning environments. There are many different ways to teach, all aimed at helping a student to learn. There are many ways to empower learners with the confidence to participate, critically and creatively, in the study of their subject area. It includes inclusive learning through promoting equality, diversity and equal opportunity, wherein institutes facilitate learning through enthusiastic and capable staff through teaching and offer other types of support for learning.

Diversity of staff and students results in different ideas, knowledge and experiences that leads to enriched learning. Treat everyone with equal dignity and worth, raising aspirations and supporting achievement for people with diverse requirements, entitlements and backgrounds. An inclusive environment for learning anticipates the varied requirements of learners like disability, specific cultural background, location, or age, and aims to ensure that all students have equal access to educational opportunities. Equality of opportunity involves enabling access for people who have differing requirements as well as eliminating arbitrary and unnecessary barriers to learning. The nature of students' particular learning experiences may vary according to the location of study, mode of study, or academic subject, as well as whether they have any protected characteristics, but every student experiences parity in the quality of learning opportunities which need to be equally accessible and inclusive, wherever possible.

According to the UK Quality Code, effective learning in higher education occurs when there is a partnership between the institutions, staff and students, and any external stakeholders, that results in teaching that aims to be inspirational, co-production and enhancement of creative and transformational learning, and a schedule of assessment that is effective both in supporting, learning and safeguarding academic standards.

4.1.1 Teaching and Support

Teaching is anything a teacher does to facilitate learning. Effective learning and teaching activities and practices are enabled through qualified staff who engage in continuing professional development, in the evaluation of their practice, and in developing their understanding of their subject and the learning process. To derive maximum learning benefit from assessment, students need to receive timely feedback in a manner that is supportive, yet includes some personal challenge. Effective feedback is the result of agreeing and communicating clear criteria before students complete the task; assessment that uses those criteria; and feedback based on the criteria and timed so that students can use it constructively in their next stage of learning. Effective feedback for learning also takes into account the need to build confidence as well as to communicate where and how improvements can be made. Effective feedback to support learning involves an ongoing dialogue between the student and staff, the student and their peers, and the student and an employer, for example, where the student is in internship. According to the UK Quality Code, institutions with their staff, students and other stakeholders, articulate and systematically review and enhance the provision of learning opportunities and teaching practices, so that every student is enabled to develop as an independent learner, study their chosen subjects in depth and enhance their capacity for analytical, critical and creative thinking.

4.1.2 Effective Learning and Teaching

As per the UK Quality Code for teaching and learning, effective learning occurs when students are enabled to engage actively in learning, and participate fully in the learning opportunities that are presented, understand their learning environment, its culture and resources, embrace the aims and expectations, demonstrate understanding of, and an ability to reflect upon, the ways in which their skills and knowledge are developing, recognise and value their existing knowledge and skills, and build upon them, make effective and responsible use of advice, guidance and feedback, avail opportunities to acquire and develop learning skills, understand sound academic practice and behave with integrity, wider experience and plans for the future, work together in an informal environment as well as in formal learning sessions, act responsibly in planning their use of the resources available to enable learning, including the effective use of their own time in independent study, give constructive feedback on their perception of the quality of their learning opportunities, engage in monitoring and influencing the curriculum, show commitment to attaining the academic standards. Topics having a broad relevance to the purposes of higher education and its wider context in society are considered in addition to subject-specific content.

4.1.3 Learning Outcomes

Opportunities for learning in higher education may be formal or informal. The learning experience involves informal learning over and above the structured formal learning. The concept of learning outcomes is applicable at all academic levels and to every subject of study. The planning and design of learning and teaching activities and associated resources provide breadth, depth, pace and challenge appropriate for the learning outcomes, subject and level of study, takes an inclusive approach and develops appropriate knowledge, skills and understanding. Achievement of learning outcomes may depend on practice and need to satisfy the requirements of a professional, statutory and regulatory body. In these situations the learning outcomes encapsulate the academic and professional competence and standards essential to the programme of study and, at the same time, are achievable by every student undertaking that programme of study. The internal quality processes assure that the learning outcomes are relevant and achievable.

Effective teaching and support for learning occurs when staff display a sound understanding and up-to-date knowledge of their subject and/or professional practice and they bring this to a variety of appropriately designed learning and teaching activities and assessment methods. They communicate enthusiasm, and draw on scholarship, research and professional activity to facilitate student learning. Effective student learning is facilitated by interaction with appropriately qualified, supported and developed teaching and support staff. Staff may be employed or visiting. Members of staff new to their teaching or enabling student learning role are encouraged to engage in appropriate induction and mentoring opportunities.

The use of technology to enhance learning can be an important means to enable students to engage fully in their programme of study. Institutions develop technological facilities and services (including virtual learning environments and library systems) that are accessible, inclusive and cater for a wide range of student requirements. Systematic consultation with students and staff about the accessibility of technological facilities enhances standards of usability. Assistive technology can make methods of learning and teaching more accessible to a wide range of students. Wherever possible, assistive technologies are made available to all students through integrated organisation-wide systems, rather than through distributed facilities or those targeted at a subset of students.

Effective teaching and learning reflect characteristics like dialogue based on mutual dignity and respect, a safe environment for exploring new ideas and for providing feedback. It also indicates whether the learning opportunities and other activities and resources are made available. Institutions actively engage students to monitor, review and evaluate this information, to ensure that it meets the requirements of different groups of students. Institutions working with their staff, students and other stakeholders, articulate, review and enhance the provision of learning opportunities and teaching practices, so that students are enabled to develop as independent learners, study their chosen subject in depth and enhance their capacity for analytical, critical and creative thinking.

4.2 LIFELONG LEARNING

The curriculum should give experience and understanding that will hopefully inculcate a desire and capability for lifelong learning. Electives have a broad relevance to the purposes of higher education and its wider context in society are considered in addition to subject-specific content. Learning and teaching activities are designed to take them into account, which may include academic and digital literacies appropriate to the academic level of the student education for sustainability, citizenship, enterprise and entrepreneurship, ethical behaviour, learning and teaching activities, practices that enable learning, and resources together enable every student who engages appropriately to achieve the learning outcomes. The learning opportunities support students to make the transition into higher education and to progress academically and intellectually.

A workshop in consultation with external experts will help build and obtain feedback towards learning outcomes, course content including visits to museums, exhibitions, monuments, research and study centres, etc., pedagogies and transaction methodologies, assessment and evaluation processes, resource persons and organisations, credits—contact classes, self-study, field visits, etc. and learning material.

4.2.1 Elective Courses

1. General Finance

   Most students don't get money management experience before they go out into the world after education to work or are self-employed. A personal, business or general finance course can teach you essential financial management skills that will serve you long after college.

2. Personality Development

   This will help deepen the student's self-understanding, build self-confidence, enhance self-social expression, team building, etc.

3. Communication

   This will help understanding of the different forms of communication including non-verbal communication. It will facilitate improved vocabulary and verbal expression, listening skills, writing, and presentation skills for social and professional interactions.

4. Critical Thinking

   This will help improve reasoning and skillful analysis, evaluation, assessment and reconstruction by providing the skillsets for organisation, correlation, interpretation and evaluation of data, information and arguments.

5. Professional Ethics and Values

   This allows students to identify, imbibe and demonstrate the significance of the moral compass, which sets the standards of personal and corporate behaviour.

6. Leadership

   This will focus on forms of leadership and the qualities and competencies that go into the making of a leader.

7. Research Methodology

   To understand principles of research and various data collection methods and analysing data to aid critical thinking.

8. Sustainability Studies

   The course will focus on human consumption, waste generation, and greenhouse effect, depletion of natural resources, population explosion, poverty and inequity. It will apply understanding on how to interact with the environment.

9. History of Art and Culture

   This course will develop an appreciation and meaning making for the art and aesthetics of various epochs and civilisations across the world based on the study of representative objects, establishing connection through visualizations with their past legacies, their present context and to their future inheritance.

10. Design Thinking

    This introduces the concept of design thinking which is iterative, synthetic, and convergent and discusses the aspects of creativity, empathy, inspiration, and ambiguity which work at the level of multiple cognitive domains—visual, mathematic, auditory, etc.

11. Creative Writing/Story Telling

    This is about appreciating the elements that go into the making of a good story. It entails learning techniques to improve writing processes and explore creativity and expression through writing. This course will also further explore cross-cultural narratives through the art of storytelling.

12. Poetry

    The serves as an introduction to understanding and appreciating poetry—its imagery, rhythm, cadence, structure and how these add up to conveying thought, feeling and experience. It will compare differing treatments of similar themes or subjects by one or more poets over one or more epochs, or track the growth and changing worldviews of a single poet over a lifetime.

13. Film Appreciation

    This course focuses on helping the students to appreciate cinema by understanding the artistic and practical elements of filmmaking, particularly how narrative and stylistic techniques are used to communicate meaning. It would also provide insight into the nature of research, exploration and technique that go into the making of a film—particularly from the perspective of costume, styling, set design and cinematography. The course would include introduction to some cinematic greats of both Indian and world cinema.

14. Theatre/Dance/Choreography/Music

    This allows students to reach their creative potential by exploring space, narrative, rhythm and movement and understand the nuances of the selected art form.

15. Sports/Fitness

    This course will engage students in-group sports/fitness activities to enable holistic development. The learning outcomes will be holistic development of the body and mind by focusing upon fitness, strength and concentration, team spirit, confidence and leadership qualities.

16. Yoga/Meditation Techniques

    This course in yoga/meditation aims at inculcating rich Indian philosophies guiding individuals to live happier and healthier lives. These techniques empower and strengthen one's body to reduce stress and become more efficient. It also promotes relaxation for clearer minds and better decision-making ability.

17. Landscaping and Gardening

    This course will give a hands-on experience of maintaining functional, aesthetically pleasing outdoor spaces. This course will also engage students in active gardening.

18. Nature/Historical Walk

    The course aims at experiential learning of the socio-cultural and historical context of the local environment. Alternatively, it will undertake walks to discover nature—flora and/or fauna in their natural habitat and explore possibilities of symbiotic relationship between humans and natural systems.

19. Psychology

    The course aims at studying the various aspects of human cognition and their impact on social behaviour. It also seeks to relate psychological theory, concepts and methods to real-life problems.

20. Economics

    This course aims at creating an understanding of core, micro and macroeconomics principles and how they apply to a wide range of real world issues.

21. Cultural Anthropology

    This course outlines the organisational principles of society, and the basis of cultural norms, mores and behaviour.

22. Sociology

    This course aims at understanding social relations, institutional structures of society and behaviour through debate, dialogue and experiential learning.

23. Media Studies

    This course will enable broad awareness and evaluation of the various forms of media and their role in the transmission of information and formation of opinion. It will study the connection between popular trends and entertainment. It will explore the impact of social media and online publishing on the media landscape and the portents for the future.

24. Photography

    This course allows students to learn the basic techniques and principles behind good photography.

25. Language

    Acquiring minimum proficiency and working knowledge in a language native to a region.

26. Systems Thinking

    This course helps to understand structural aspects and consequent behaviour of systems arising out of interrelatedness, feedback loops, self-organising behaviour and the emergent, dynamic nature of systems.

27. Nutrition

    Nutrition is a topic that is both interesting and good for your health. It teaches biology and food science while exploring how the foods affects body.

5
Quality Evaluation

Effective means of evaluation are required for ensuring dissemination of quality education and learning and diffusion of educational innovation to the community. The current methods of evaluation in HE do not promote effective learning. For innovative dissemination of knowledge which is the need of the hour, an active and visible support to encourage and support innovation and good practices can be established by developing acceptable and practicable systems for evaluation. For ensuring quality learning, recognizing development of acceptable formative methods is necessary. Institutions need to be concerned and mandate for effective evaluation methods and user-based evaluation. If institutions refine procedures to improve validity and reliability, effective evaluation should occur.

A method for evaluating courses, teaching and learning in higher education is sorely required by educational institutes to deliver quality education. The four major components for developing a system for this are approach to teaching, delivery of teaching, outcomes of teaching and recognition of the academic. Evaluation of teaching and learning initiative needs to be encouraged through the use of formative and summative evaluations that focus on investigating links between the particular objectives of initiatives and educational outcomes. Provision of professional development and support programmes that focus on educational evaluation as well as teaching tools and methodologies is required.

The chapter overviews the methods for effective evaluation and user-based evaluation; while recognizing the need of evaluation for certification; and by engaging students in the process; to make them effective lifelong learners. It also addresses the benefits of formative assessment and importance of continuous evaluation. The chapter evaluates the methods, procedures and strategies for effective and thorough and user-based evaluation of learning, while recognizing the need for certification. It also overviews the importance of internal assessment and continuous evaluation, using subjective and objective elements and recommends various reforms. It addresses the benefits of formative assessment and recommends its implementation. It expresses the need for students to become effective lifelong learners by engaging in the evaluation through feedback from peers, practitioners and others which will enable them to undertake subsequent learning effectively.

Areas addressed by the initiatives identified for learner-based outcomes include student retention and student engagement, enhancing learning, catering for groups of students with diverse skills, accommodating large class sizes, curriculum integration and teaching skills associated with professional practice.

5.1 CRITERIA FOR EVALUATION

> Examinations are formidable even to the best prepared, for the greatest fool may ask more than the wisest man can answer.
>
> —*Charles Colton*

An examination is certainly a mechanism for the assessment of a student's performance and future potential. Another major advantage of the examination system is that it sets a time-frame and an achievable set of objectives for students. By setting goals, the students are motivated to achieve clearly-defined levels of learning and competence. For the students, examinations provide an opportunity to manage time, plan and direct their effort to achieve specific educational and development goals. A systematic approach is required in which the milestones are the various evaluation components. Or else the student may well end up spending his or her effort in an undirected manner and not achieving his or her full potential.

In this way, the examination system moulds the student to a work culture which later helps him or her to become a productive and valuable member of the economy. With an increasing change towards a 'knowledge-based economy', the importance of this type of work culture will increase greatly. We cannot doubt that this culture has in part moulded the characters—and therefore the careers—of brilliant performers in the global IT and financial sectors who have received at least the early part of their college education in India.

But with the current system in existence, it is brought forth in most of the studies that the student's effort throughout the education is concentrated almost wholly on how to get through the examination. Students concentrate only on the test and beating it which is not helpful in learning. If any activity is not related directly or indirectly to the examination, it fails to evoke or enlist their enthusiasm. They are interested in methods which secure an easy pass rather than those which are educationally sound. It is necessary to make intangible efforts for character building, well-rounded personality, a wholesome emotional and social development, physical and mental health, social adjustment and a proper development of appreciation of the finer values in life. It is much easier to show results in intellectual attainments and academic progress.

The attitude of the parents also lends support to this state of affairs. Because of the close connection between employment and the passing of examinations, the average parent is more interested in his child passing that examination than in anything else. Even the authorities who provide higher courses or employ young people are guided almost solely by the certificates awarded on the results of the external examinations. To this may be added the unfortunate trend to utilize the marks obtained at public examinations as the sole criterion for admission of students to most institutions.

Taking into consideration the above, it is necessary for institutions to continuously assess the learning instead of only one examination. Continuous assessment definitely contributes to better education and assessment. The proposed framework should include computer-based examination, analysis/design focus and practical examination along with the written examination which can present with different and complementary means of assessing a student's learning and ability. The practical examination of a student should include specially designed experiments to test knowledge of basics, as well as practical skills demonstrable in the laboratory. The aim of an oral examination should be to test the student's understanding of basic concepts, and ability to express in simple and clear language.

With proper division of work and planning, and with the use of Information Technology, results should be declared timely. Apart from fairness and reliability, the timeliness of results is an important criterion of the performance of an evaluation system. It should be possible for a student to review answer-books to have fairness in the system.

The evaluation system should include both the subjective element along with the objective part side by side. The questions should discourage cramming and encourage intelligent understanding. Semester pattern of examination with a system of continuous learning and evaluation is required. A semester evaluation may include three assignments which judge the subject mastery, first semester, mid semester and semester end—three examinations. The cumulative of the semester grade point may be carried forward to the last semester.

5.2 EFFECTIVE CREDIT AND EVALUATION SYSTEMS

The marking system should be replaced with an effective grading system. A good grading system must meet three criteria: it should accurately reflect differences in student performance, it should be clear to students so they can chart their own progress, and it should be fair. Performance can be defined either in relative or absolute terms (comparing students with each other or measuring their achievement against a set scale), and each system has its defenders. But whichever grading scheme one uses, students should be able to calculate (at least roughly) how they are doing in the course at any point in the semester. Some relative grading schemes make it impossible for students to estimate their final grades because the cutoff points in the final distribution are not determined until the end of the course.

A complete description of the grading system should appear in the course syllabus, including the amount of credit for each assignment, how the final grades will be calculated, and the grade equivalents for the final scores.

Also, students should perceive the grading system as fair and equitable, rewarding them proportionately for their achievements. From the standpoint of measurement, many different kinds of assignments, spread over the entire semester provide a fairer estimate of student learning than one or two large tests.

Some of grading systems followed all over the world are given below.

5.2.1 European Universities

The European Course Credit Transfer System has 60 credits representing the workload of a year of study.

Table 5.1: European Credit System

A	Excellent	outstanding performance with only minor errors
B	Very good	above the average standard but with some errors
C	Good	generally sound work with a number of notable errors
D	Satisfactory	fair but with significant shortcomings
E	Sufficient	performance meets the minimum criteria
FX	Fail	considerable further work required before credit can be awarded
F	Fail	considerable further work is required

5.2.2 American Universities

American universities employ a system of continuous assessment and assign grades for each course taken. Almost everything you do for a class will influence final grade. Examinations and tests, essays or written assignments, laboratory reports, laboratory or studio work, class attendance, and class participation may all be used to determine your final grade. This means it is essential to keep up with the reading and course work and to attend classes on a regular basis. The following is a general percentage/letter grade scale for classes taken at US colleges:

Table 5.2: US Credit System

A	100 to 90 %
B	89 to 80 %
C	79 to 70 %
D	69 to 60 %
E	59 to 50 %
F	49 to 0 %

5.2.3 Dutch Universities

Based on the European Course Credit Transfer System (ECTS), the full study load for one year is 60 EC, where 1 credit is equivalent to 28 hours of study. The grading system is based on a number scale from 1 (very poor) to 10 (outstanding). The lowest passing grade is 6. A 10 is rarely awarded.

Table 5.3: Dutch Credit System

1	Very Poor
6	Passing
10	Outstanding

5.2.4 Australia—Queens' University

Table 5.4: Australian Credit System

80 to 100 per cent	Grade A	Exam deferred	ED
65 to 79 per cent	Grade B	Aggregate grade	AG
50 to 64 per cent	Grade C	Credit	CR
Below 50 per cent	Grade F	Audit only	AU
Final examination not written	NW	Dropped	DR
Coursework incomplete	IN	In progress	IP
Grade deferred*	GD		

5.2.5 The Danish Grading System—13 Point Scale

Table 5.5: Danish Credit System

13	The exceptionally independent and excellent performance
11	The independent and excellent performance
10	The excellent but not particularly independent performance
9	The good performance a little above average
8	The average performance

7	The mediocre performance, slightly below average
6	The just acceptable performance/passed
5	The hesitant and not satisfactory performance/not passed
3	The very hesitant, very insufficient and unsatisfactory performance/not passed
0	The completely unacceptable performance, hesitant/not passed

5.2.6 German Grading System

Table 5.6: German Credit System

1.00 - 1.50	A	Very Good
1.51 - 2.00	A-	Good
2.01 – 2.50	B+	Good
2.51 - 3.00	B	Satisfactory
3.01 – 3.50	B-	Satisfactory
3.51 – 4.00	C	Adequate
4.01 – 4.50	D	Adequate
Below 4.50		Fail

5.2.7 Virginia International University Grading System

Table 5.7: Virginian Credit System

A	4.0 Excellent 4.0 grade points per credit	95-100
A-	3.7	90-94
B+	3.3	85-89
B	3.0	80-84
B-	2.7	75-79
C+	2.3	70-74
C	2.0 Average/Satisfactory 2.0 grade point per credit	65-69
C-	1.7	60-64
D+	1.3	55-59
D	1.0	50-54
D-	0.7 Lowest Passing Grade	45-49
F	0.0 Failure or Unofficial Withdrawal 0.0 grade point per credit	0-44
I	Incomplete	
P	Pass	

S	Satisfactory	
U	Unsatisfactory	
R	Re-enroll	
W	Withdrawal	

5.3 STUDENTS' PARTICIPATION IN EVALUATION

The most important characteristic for any successful evaluation method is validity—whether a procedure measures what it purports to measure. It becomes inappropriate, meaningless, and useless to make specific inferences from invalid measurements. Evidence of validity must be accumulated to support inferences made from evaluation results. Successful evaluation methods also must be reliable, effective, and efficient (Wise and others, 1984). Reliability means consistency—an evaluation always must give similar scores, ranking, or ratings for similar tests, regardless of the evaluator or the evaluated. Effectiveness implies that the evaluation provides results in their most useful format. Summative evaluation yields a score or rank that does not have to be interpreted to be used for accountability. Formative evaluation initiates the improvement of weak areas. Efficiency refers to spending time and money for evaluation training, materials, and procedure to ensure the desired results. To evaluate learning and quality of education, adoption of standard-based framework for evaluation is necessary by prohibiting norm-referenced evaluation. This will help students to realize whether their achievements are a result of meeting an acceptable standard or simply doing better than others in the same cohort. Students must always be treated as if they will succeed. To admit students and assume they will not succeed is ethically irresponsible. If this is not a valid reason the intake should change. Evaluation must contribute towards building confidence in the ability of the students to learn. Grading and feedback should be separated. Grades classify work which binds learner to this and cannot point effectively to improvement. Greater emphasis should be on students' learning and understanding rather than performance goals.

The following components can be used in combination for involving students in evaluation.

5.3.1 Feedback from Students

As the intended beneficiaries of the educational system, students are in a unique position to help their teachers in the evaluation process. Who else could possibly answer these kinds of questions better than the students themselves? Of all the sources of information, students are the best source for understanding the immediate effects of the process of teaching and learning.

5.3.2 Questionnaires

The most common method of obtaining student reactions is to use a questionnaire. The special value of questionnaires is that they obtain responses from everyone and they allow for an anonymous and a candid response. The limitation is that they can only ask a question once, i.e., that cannot probe for further clarification. The questionnaires at the beginning of a course can be used to get information about the students, e.g., prior course work or experience with the subject, preferred modes of teaching and learning, and special problems a student might have. Mid-term questionnaires get an early warning of any existing problems so that changes can be made in time to benefit this set of students. The advantage of end-of-term questionnaires, which is common practice, is that all the learning activities have been completed. Consequently, students can respond meaningfully to questions about the overall effectiveness of the course. Questionnaires can be developed in-house or those developed for evaluation nationally/internationally can be used.

5.3.3 Interviews

The other well-established way of finding out about student reactions is to talk to them. Either the teacher (if sufficient trust and rapport exists) or an outside person (if more anonymity and objectivity are desired) can talk with students about the course, teaching and learning. The special value of interviews is that students often identify unanticipated strengths and weaknesses, and the interviewer can probe and follow-up on topics that need clarification. The limitation of course is that a teacher can usually interview only a few students. A teacher can informally get responses many times. Although the students know better than anyone what their own reactions are, they can also be biased and limited in their own perspectives. Perhaps more significantly, students usually do not have a full understanding of how a course might be taught, either in terms of pedagogy or content. Hence, they can effectively address what is, but not what might be.

5.3.4 Students' Performance

Teachers almost always give students some form of graded exercise, whether it is an in-class test or an out-of-class project. Usually, though, the intent of the test is to assess the quality of student learning. One can also use this same information to assess the quality of teaching and programme. Feedback is much more effective in letting students and the teacher know whether they are learning what they need to learn as the course goes along. Some students work very hard in a course, not because the teacher inspires or motivates them but because they require a good grade in the course. Therefore, they work hard to learn it on their own.

5.3.5 Peer Review

Colleagues observe each other's learning; examine lessons, tests, and assignments. Peer review examines a wider scope of learning activities than other methods. Disadvantages include time consumption and possible peer conflict. Formative application features may justify the time demands and minimize sources of tension.

5.3.6 Outside Observer

In addition to the two parties directly involved in a course, the teacher and the students, valuable information can be obtained from the observations of a third party, someone who brings both an outsider's perspective and professional expertise to the task. Part of the value of an outside observer is that they do not have a personal stake in the particular course; hence they are free to reach positive and negative conclusions without any cost to themselves. Also, as a professional, they can bring an expertise either in content and/or in pedagogy that is likely to supplement that of both the teacher and the students. A variety of kinds of observers exist: a peer colleague, a senior colleague, or an instructional specialist. Faculty members should consider inviting one or more outside observers to their classes at least once a semester for two or three years. They need to get as many new perspectives on teaching as soon as possible. Again, the strength of being an outsider is also its weakness. Outside observers can usually only visit one or two class sessions and therefore do not know what happens in the rest of the course. Apart from this general problem, each kind of observer has its own limitation. The peer colleague may also have limited experience and perspectives; the senior colleague may be someone who makes departmental decisions about annual evaluations and tenure; and the instructional consultant may have limited knowledge of the subject matter.

5.3.7 Benchmarking and Monitoring

A very effective way is to compare and contrast approaches with similar institutions. To gain the benefits of benchmarking requires an exchange of detailed information which can be analysed in depth. Continuous monitoring of the teaching and learning process and a formal recording of information can be carried out throughout the learning process by the institution. This will help ensure whether the course objectives and the teaching and learning objectives comply to established standards.

5.3.8 Feedback from Community

The views of a representative sample can be taken by encouraging feedback from a cross section of the community through surveys, focus groups, representation, etc. about the learning and evaluation patterns followed in the institute.

5.3.9 Self-Evaluation

This method usually supplements more formal evaluation methods and is used with other data to identify the weak areas and overcome them. While feedback generally originates from a teacher, learners can also play an important role in formative assessment through self-evaluation.

5.3.10 Indirect Measures

Other issues can be examined to determine if they correlate with student achievement. These descriptors include enthusiasm, humor, judgment, objectivity, and punctuality.

Information Technology use needs to be explored in the form of online surveys which can be an efficient way of collecting data particularly in a well-developed network which offers connectivity to all students and teachers.

5.4 CONCEPT OF FORMATIVE ASSESSMENT

While many educators are highly focused on tests, it is important to consider that over the year, teachers can build in many opportunities to assess how students are learning and then use this information to make beneficial changes. This diagnostic use of assessment to provide feedback to teachers and students over the course of instruction is called formative assessment. It stands in contrast to summative assessment, which generally takes place after a period of instruction and requires making a judgment about the learning that has occurred (e.g. by grading or scoring a test or paper). Formative type of evaluation on the other hand guides in how to learn what they wish to learn and tells us how well they are progressing to get there. It is neither possible nor desirable to remove the summative judgements of others but a shift is required to equip students to sustain as lifelong evaluators.

Black and William (1998) define assessment broadly to include all activities that teachers and students undertake to get information that can be used diagnostically to alter teaching and learning. Under this definition, assessment encompasses teacher observation, classroom discussion, and analysis of student work, including homework and tests. Assessments become formative when the information is used to adapt teaching and learning to meet student needs. When teachers know how students are progressing and where they are having trouble, they can use this information to make necessary instructional adjustments, such as re-teaching, trying alternative instructional approaches, or offering more opportunities for practice. These activities can lead to improved student success.

After an extensive research review of 250 journal articles and book chapters to determine whether formative assessment raises academic standards in the classroom, they concluded that efforts to strengthen formative assessment produce significant learning gains as measured by comparing the average improvements in the test scores of the students involved in the innovation with the range of scores found for typical groups of students on the same tests. Formative assessment apparently helped low-achieving students, including students with learning disabilities, even more than it helped other students. It helps learners become aware of any gaps that exist between their desired goal and their current knowledge, understanding, or skill and guides them through actions necessary to obtain the goal by specific comments about errors and specific suggestions for improvement and encourages students to focus their attention thoughtfully on the task.

Black and William (1998) encourage teachers to use questioning and classroom discussion as an opportunity to increase their students' knowledge and improve understanding. They caution, however, that teachers need to make sure to ask thoughtful, reflective questions rather than simple, factual ones and then give students adequate time to respond. In order to involve everyone, they suggest strategies such as the following:

- Invite students to discuss their thinking about a question or topic in pairs or small groups, then ask a representative to share their thinking with the larger group (sometimes called think-pair-share).
- Present several possible answers to a question, then ask students to vote on them.
- Ask all students to write down an answer, and then read a selected few out loud.

Teachers might also assess students' understanding in the following ways:

- Have students write their understanding of vocabulary or concepts before and after instruction?
- Ask students to summarize the main ideas they've taken away from a lecture, discussion, or assigned reading.
- Have students complete a few problems or questions at the end of instruction and check answers?
- Interview students individually or in groups about their thinking as they solve problems.

- Assign brief, in-class writing assignments (e.g. Why is this person or event representative of this time period in history?).

In addition to these classroom techniques, tests and homework can be used formatively if teachers analyze where students are in their learning and provide specific, focused feedback regarding performance and ways to improve it. Black and William (1998) make the following recommendations:

- Frequent short tests are better than infrequent long ones.
- New learning should be tested within about a week of first exposure.
- Be mindful of the quality of test items and work with other teachers and outside sources to collect good ones.

Portfolios, or collections of student work, may also be used formatively if students and teachers annotate the entries and observe growth over time and practice (Duschl and Gitomer, 1997). Formative assessment is tightly linked with instructional practices. Teachers need to consider how their classroom activities, assignments, and tests supports learning aims and allow students to communicate what they know, then use this information to improve teaching and learning.

Teachers generally need to undertake or participate in some summative assessment as a basis for reporting grades or meeting accountability standards. However, the task of summative assessment remains quite different from the task of formative assessment to monitor and improve progress. While tests provide a snapshot of a student's performance on a given day under test conditions, formative assessment allows teachers to monitor and guide students' performance over time in multiple problem-solving situations.

5.5 LEARNER-BASED EVALUATION

> The authority to those who teach is often an obstacle to those who want to learn.
>
> —*Cicero*

Evaluation needs to encompass the abilities required to undertake activities that necessarily accompany learning throughout life in formal and informal settings. Evaluation involves identifying appropriate standards and making judgements about quality. The present evaluation systems are controlled by the knowledge givers like teachers, educational institutions and professional bodies. It gives responsibility of education to them. The educational institutions have become obsessed with certification and grading and public measures of performance and accountability. The evaluation systems drive off learning while at the same time seek to measure it. Evaluation therefore needs to move from the exclusive domain of evaluators to learners. It should be sustainable in nature that meets the needs of the present and prepares students to meet future learning needs.

In a learning society learners adopt a learning approach to life, drawing on a wide range of lifestyle practices. Learners today will continue to be learners throughout their lives more than ever before. It is the responsibility of educators to equip all learners for formal and informal learning. This requires going beyond course-related goals and view learning and evaluation in a wider term. The students need to be prepared not just for the outcome of the course but to operate in a complex society. Frequent self-evaluation is highly efficacious in enhancing student achievement. Peer evaluation can also help if encouraged in the right perspective. The challenge is to find a balance between providing a wide range of new learning opportunities for students and enabling them to complete the feedback loop enough times for them to gain confidence that their achievements are secure and can really demonstrate the desired outcomes.

In order to equip students for a learning society, we must not only provide suitable forms of formative assessment as part of any learning enterprise, but we must also find ways of embedding formative assessment thinking into all acts of learning. Learners should be able to undertake their own processes using whatever resources they can identify using colleagues, peers and friends and other sources. Consideration of standards and criteria is not enough in itself unless they are applied to learner's own work and feedback sought on the appropriateness of the application, then learners cannot be confident that they are able to use them to improve their own learning.

The students need to know how they are progressing in the direction desired for which a range of strategies and devices need to be developed which can be used in learning such as setting of intermediate goals checking progress at regular intervals to sophisticated cognitive devices. Students should be exposed to certain kinds of questions in evaluation so that they may be able to develop the ability to discern and handle simultaneously the relevant aspects of various situations. The aim is to be engaged in discerning pertinent aspects of problems or issues and finding ways to simultaneously handle them. To do this, students need to draw upon both disciplinary and professional knowledge.

Students need access to learning peers and others with expertise to reflect on challenges and gain support for renewed efforts. Peers are required to help check our understanding, see alternate ways of interpreting a task or situation, give ideas, provide support when feeling low, identify new sources of information and provide other views and judgements. In educational institutes, there are never enough teachers around when needed to provide this range of expertise and they are not necessarily the most useful persons to provide it.

Unless feedback is applied and used to demonstrate improvements, there is no way to tell if it has been effective. Lifelong learners need to be mindful of the language they use to refer to their own learning and do not use excessive judgmental language. Self-oppression is often more difficult to extract oneself from than oppression from a known external source. The students if not engaged in the construction and reconstruction of criteria for judging work, they will not be able to effectively establish criteria for work. If they only write essays, they may not be able to communicate in other modes. If they only learn to perform in unseen examinations, they may not be able to deploy the range of resources of the normal work environment. If they only write theory, they won't know how to put ideas into practice. And so on.

Teachers need to be more transparent about their own expertise and what constitutes it, and make their knowledge available to learners. This can be done by enlisting students in the process of how to come to know what they know. A move towards great openness in standards requires an attempt to be more explicit. Students should not be deprived of information concerning assessment weightings or course objectives, a further move to explicate and make accessible the standards in marking assignments and judging good work is needed. Teachers must learn to focus on their expertise as learners and decentre their role as possessors of knowledge.

5.6 ASPECTS OF EVALUATION

Evaluation for lifelong learning is not a method or technique, but a way of thinking about all aspects of evaluation. Evaluation can have very positive and negative effects and has an impact on all. It influences learning, and it helps construct the society. All aspects of assessment involve more than is apparent and must be judged accordingly. Unless the thinking and practice is part of the curriculum at all levels, students will not be equipped for lifelong learning.

The students need to be equipped for effective evaluation, learn self-assessment strategies, understanding and setting criteria, ability in identifying cues and clues from the context of learning, making appropriate judgements, giving and receiving feedback. Institute-wide policies about evaluation will be accepted widely, the translation of it into practice needs to take account of many factors. It requires an appreciation of them and how they are manifest in any particular cause, faculty or location as well as how wider contextual influences impact on student learning.

The potential unintended effects need to be spotted before an assessment strategy is adopted. This involves, firstly examining the effects of assessment on students' approaches to learning, whether this form of assessment tends to encourage students to take a deep approach to learning. And, secondly to examine the effects of the assessment on students' approaches to evaluation. It should encourage students to meaningfully engage with criteria for good work in the area and add to student's repertoire of self-assessment strategies. It should also prompt students to devise their own assessment strategies to better respond to the assessment tasks set.

6
Engaging Students

Student engagement can be conceptualised as individual and collective participation and passionate involvement of students in curricular, co-curricular and extra-curricular activities and interactions (Singh and Srivastava, 2013). The concept of student involvement was coined by Astin (1984) and he used the term for curricular and extra-curricular domains. The quality of education can be defined in terms of the achievement of learning outcomes. The students avail the opportunities to develop themselves academically, socially, culturally and professionally. Interestingly, students show a varied degree of involvement in learning and development opportunities (Singh and Srivastava, 2013). Student engagement needs to be embedded as a part of institutional philosophy and practice. A proper structure to accommodate students at all levels with regular monitoring and review of engagement activities need to be carried out and documented. A student engagement audit is needed to review the activities, professionals and resources and the level of the student participation. Exploring areas for maximum student engagement and improving upon it is the only way forward to ensure high quality of education are vital to strengthen the quality of education.

The United Kingdom and Scotland have a Quality Code which clearly defines the expectations for student engagement from educational institutions which are given below, and as defined by the Quality Assurance Agency (QAA). Student engagement in quality is central to the approach in Scotland and embedded in its culture. Students are at the heart of the system and they involve them as partners. They play an active role in supporting student engagement, through the inclusion of student members in all review teams, through student involvement in the enhancement themes, and as members of committees and working groups. Based on this expectation can be set for the educational institutions in India for enhancing and monitoring quality.

6.1 STUDENT ENGAGEMENT

Student engagement in education needs to be irrespective of location, discipline, mode of study, teaching delivery, etc. Its focus should be on the provision of an inclusive environment for student engagement, as indicated by the QAA. The environment should anticipate varied needs of learners and aims to ensure that all students have equal access to educational opportunities. It is the time spent on a task; quality of effort; student involvement; social and academic integration; good practices in education; and learning outcomes. The term covers two domains as per the QAA relating to:

- improving the motivation of students to engage in learning and to learn independently,
- the participation of students in quality enhancement and quality assurance processes, resulting in the improvement of their educational experience.

It includes but may not be restricted to representation of the student view through formal representation mechanisms. It needs to be widely accepted that the views of students, individually and collectively, should inform quality systems with the purpose of improving the student educational experience both for current and future cohorts. Student involvement in quality can have a positive influence on the delivery and development of any aspect of the student educational experience, a faculty, a department, or an individual member of staff. As per the QAA, aspects of the educational journey into which students can offer insight include:

- application and admission
- induction
- programme and curriculum design, delivery

- curriculum content
- teaching delivery
- learning opportunities
- learning resources
- student support and guidance
- assessment
- governance

All students should have the opportunity to be involved in quality enhancement and assurance processes in a manner and at a level appropriate to them. In considering approaches it is important that higher education institutes create a culture and environment where students are encouraged to take up the opportunities on offer. For this environment to be effective, QAA expects that higher education institutions should:

- foster active student participation in their quality systems, including using individual and collective feedback from students,
- implement transparent mechanisms, agreed with students, for the nomination and election of student representatives,
- provide induction and ongoing support for students and staff appropriate to their quality assurance roles,
- monitor, review and enhance the effectiveness of their policies and processes for engaging students in quality processes.

They should partner related to joint working between students and staff, based on the values of openness; trust and honesty; agreed shared goals and values; and regular communication. It is based on legitimate, but different, perceptions and experiences rather than equal responsibility and liability. By working together to a common agreed purpose, steps can be taken that lead to enhancements for all concerned. The terms reflect a mature relationship based on mutual respect between students and staff. Partnership working can occur both in informal and formal arrangements, including representation mechanisms involving a students' association.

Both higher education institutions and students benefit through the practice of working both with individuals and representatives. HEIs have different missions, operate in different contexts, and have student populations that differ in composition and demographics. They tailor their educational offering to meet their mission and the needs of their student population. How each education institute defines student engagement is therefore likely to differ.

HEIs, in partnership with their student body, should define and promote the range of opportunities for any student to engage in educational enhancement and quality assurance. HE is not a passive process—it is transformational for the individual, as well as having transactional elements. HEIs promote active involvement by students in all aspects of their learning and provide opportunities for students to influence their individual and collective learning journey. The nature of opportunities for students to engage in formal and informal quality systems varies between HEIs, as well as by programme, academic and organisational level (institute, faculty or department; or programme, module or individual). Once education institutes have agreed their definition of student engagement with their student body, opportunities are promoted widely to students and staff, and student engagement is embedded in the HEI's quality policies, processes and practices, as per the UK Quality Code.

A definition of student engagement may be communicated via a student charter, or similar document. Education institutes engage the student body in an active and timely way. They accord the same importance to early engagement with the student body, for example, during the design phase of a new curriculum, as it does to having student representation at the formal programme approval or as part of periodic programme review. HEIs should ensure that students are supported and informed in order to provide feedback that is effective and useful to the HEI. HEIs work with the student body to develop solutions that address issues arising from that feedback. Subsequently, students are informed of the actions that have taken place to encourage further future engagement.

HEIs should devise effective ways of communicating to students when and where their feedback has been acted upon, or where change is not possible, the reasons why this has not happened. This is often referred to as 'closing the feedback loop'.

Students appreciate engagement opportunities timed so that they experience a direct benefit as a result of their input, in addition to the benefits provided for succeeding cohorts. For this reason, HEIs need to develop a framework for eliciting comments from students that employs a range of methods, that is timely, not overly onerous, and of demonstrable direct benefit to the students providing the feedback.

Mechanisms for involving students as per the QAA may include:

- questionnaires; for example, at the end of a module or year
- student representative structures
- research activities; for example, through focus groups
- student membership of committees
- student consultation events
- student involvement in projects
- student dialogue with decision makers
- online discussion forums
- formal quality processes; for example, periodic programme review.

HEIs should make available opportunities for individual feedback, including feedback provided anonymously (for example, through student evaluations or suggestion boxes), as well as opportunities for collective feedback through student representation systems. It is important that whatever the mechanisms used for involving students, they are not 'one-off' initiatives but are undertaken as part of a sustained strategy of student involvement.

6.2 VALUING THE CONTRIBUTIONS

HEIs need to recognise the value of the engagement of their students and ensure that students feel rewarded for their involvement. Working in partnership with the student body, they should develop ways to recognise the efforts of their students and the skills they develop through taking on roles. The UGC should set out expectations about student engagement seeking that the education institutes take deliberate steps to engage students, individually and collectively, as partners in the assurance and enhancement of their educational experience. HEIs, in partnership with their student body, define and promote the range of opportunities for any student to engage in educational enhancement and quality assurance. That the HEIs create and maintain an environment within which students and staff engage in discussions that aim to bring about demonstrable enhancement of the educational experience. They should share information regarding the results of internal and external student questionnaires and other forms of feedback, such as the analyses of student performance at module and programme level, reports from professional, statutory and regulatory bodies, employability information and reports of actions taken by the institute to enhance the student educational experience.

Students and staff should engage in evidence-based discussions based on the mutual sharing of information, as per the UK Quality Code. Staff and students to disseminate and jointly recognise the enhancements made to the student educational experience, and the efforts of students in achieving these successes. The effectiveness of student engagement should be monitored and reviewed annually, using pre-defined key performance indicators, and policies and processes enhanced where required. Performance indicators may consider aspects such as the effectiveness of systems, progress in engaging all groups, and outcomes in relation to demonstrable enhancements to the educational experience as a result of student engagement.

6.3 EFFECTIVE REPRESENTATION

Arrangements should exist for the effective representation structures for collective student voice and diversity amongst them at all organisational levels, and these arrangements should provide opportunities for all students to be heard. HEIs should use effective student representation in decision-making processes including on governing boards and senior committees at institute, faculty and departmental level. HEIs should ensure that student representatives and staff have access to training and ongoing support to equip them to fulfil their roles in educational enhancement and quality assurance effectively.

7

Appeals, Complaints and Mentoring

7.1 APPEALS AND COMPLAINTS

The UK Quality Code defines an academic appeal as a request for a review of a decision of an academic body charged with making decisions on student progression, assessment and awards. It defines a complaint as the expression of a specific concern about matters that affect the quality of a student's learning opportunities. Appeals or complaints may be made by individual students or, collectively by groups of students. In designing and implementing procedures for appeals and complaints, the need to eliminate discrimination; harassment and victimisation; to advance equality of opportunity; and to foster good relations are high on consideration. It needs to be ensured that procedures apply equally to all students.

Effective resolution of appeals and complaints is possible if the staff and students are concerned enough to look into the same with objectivity and respect. An outcome which is not favourable is acceptable if the process has been designed and implemented in a way which is fair and based on evidence, rejecting complaints that are vexatious. Students lodging an appeal or complaint should feel safe in doing so and protected from being at a disadvantage and being inhibited. Information, advice and guidance is provided to students and staff at each stage of the process.

It is difficult to distinguish between appeals and complaints since both adhere to be similar. It also involves opportunities for resolution through mediation or less formal means which are additional or separate. Time limits for different processes and stages need to be clarified. Learning from cases irrespective of the outcome of the individual case, independent review, fair, accessible and timely procedures enable enhancement.

7.1.1 Appeal and Complaint Guidelines

It should be made clear to whom the procedures apply to—current students, students on approved leave and students who have recently left their programme. Information about the procedures and responsibilities should be transparent. To whom an appeal or complaint must be directed, who would be involved in considering such an appeal or complaint, review of complaints, etc. Collective complaints management should be fair representing the views of all. Issues of confidentiality and disclosure and whether anonymous complaints will be considered should be placed in the procedures.

Constructive engagement and opportunities for early and/or informal resolution and engagement in a spirit of cooperation promotes confidence, fairness and objectivity in procedures. Clear processes, not potentially intimidating, provide students with appropriate opportunities to provide relevant evidence. Where students see action was taken previously, builds trust and confidence in the process. Alternative means for resolving complaints may help to achieve earlier resolution and need to be informed, including impartial mediation. Complaints that are resolved through such alternative arrangements and how recurring issues can be identified and acted on are detailed. Procedures are written in a way that is easily accessible and clear to students. Equality, diversity, barriers to access are taken into account. Any changes are brought to the attention of the students and staff in a timely manner. The scope and grounds for appeals are not clearly stated.

Clear and accurate advice and guidance is available for an appeal or complaint, and for staff involved in handling them. Students can make informed decisions about whether and how to lodge an appeal or complaint, and therefore make effective use of the applicable procedures. Details on advocacy and support provisions are specified.

As proposed in the UK Quality Code, handling appeals and complaints is specialized. Induction and briefing, and opportunities for professional updating are provided, including need for impartiality, appropriate approaches to handling evidence and witnesses, issues of confidentiality and data protection, etc. Academic appeals and complaints procedures are conducted in a timely and fair manner, including being proportionate, allowing for objective and impartial consideration, and allowing all parties to engage on equal footing. The following may be considered:

- Avoiding unreasonable delay at various stages may be cut down by defining time periods
- Relevant guidance on good practice is available along stages
- How to determine whether grounds exist for appeal or complaint, and provide opportunity to challenge the finding
- Authority for final decision and appeals process
- Unacceptable behaviour, and its consequences
- Relating procedures to relevant professional, statutory or regulatory bodies
- The impact on procedures in case of legal intervention during the proceedings.

7.1.2 Appeals and Complaints Procedures

- face to face meetings where the absence of such provision might be considered unfair
- alternative arrangements
- specialist advice
- managing proceedings in a timely manner
- informing the student of any right to attend, any right to be accompanied or represented, and any rights to submit evidence or witnesses

- provide equal access to all the evidence that will be used as a basis for determining the outcome.

Ensure that appropriate action is taken. Effective outcomes give clear reasons for reaching the decision which students can understand. This helps the student determine whether or not to pursue the matter further. Where an appeal or complaint is upheld, explain how and when they will implement any remedy, and whether that might include an apology. Student is provided with a clear written statement on completion of internal procedures, advise any relevant external procedures to which they have recourse.

Monitor and evaluate the effectiveness of appeals and complaints procedures, reflect on the outcomes for enhancement purposes. Monitoring how procedures work overall and maintaining records of such monitoring over time, ensures that procedures are fair and are working. In order to monitor operation effectively, record appeals and complaints, and consider the extent to which it is possible or appropriate to monitor alternative means of resolution.

Reporting and evaluation also assists while reviewing periodically the conduct of procedures. Such reviews, which engage students in the process of review, with legislative requirements and good practice enables to gather valuable feedback for enhancement purposes. The provision of information to staff and students on the actions taken helps to raise awareness of the procedures and build confidence of students and staff in transparency and effectiveness.

7.2 ACADEMIC MENTORING

Mentoring is giving advice or helping students in their academic journey. The process of mentoring is seen as a supportive, informal, and individualized activity. Academic mentoring is about understanding academic inclinations. It is done by an experienced teacher. Mentoring helps improve job prospects through improved time management skills, motivation, study and self-confidence, which help give better academic results. There are many opportunities in universities which the student can build upon but they may be missed by students once they get into the routine university life. Mentors challenge and support with such activities. University provides freedom to the students and it makes it difficult for parents. Mentors challenge students to look more critically in what they are doing. Mentor is a trusted adviser and counsel for any issues the student would like to discuss. Self-awareness and purpose is what the students should gain.

Mentors act as role models and spend time with students once or twice a week and encourage them, listen, suggest, take them to events, activities, to help students learn about their career and further education. The students mentee are guided through the choices to be made in the course of the programme regarding specializations, electives, internship, etc., as well as build up a relationship that assists to identify academic strengths and weaknesses in a less formal setting outside the context of the classroom, which permits greater openness and help them achieve career paths that are suitable to the strengths and aptitude. A good mentor will be able to help the mentees recognize their skill sets based on their potential and interests to choose their career pathways accordingly. The mentors will have to guide the students and ensure that they make appropriate choices, through myriad ways.

7.2.1 Types of Mentoring

- Subject Mentor - One to one, group mentoring
- Academic Mentor - Group mentoring, one of one mentoring
- E-Mentor - FAQs (for students and faculty) on CMS

7.2.2 Mentoring Ways

The different ways of academic mentoring are:

1. One to One Mentoring. The academic mentors meet the students individually on one to one basis. This generally involves more time to be spent with the mentee. Department assigns mentors to students. Certain hours per week are assigned for mentoring which include:

- Choice of specialization, electives
- Subject mentoring (assessment and guidance on strengths and weakness)
- Internship
- Project

The mentor will be introduced to the students during the orientation and help on their choices, according to individual interests. They will oversee the overall professional development of the students, including time management, attendance and grades. They will maintain student-wise journals, encapsulating the feedback given.

2. Group Mentoring. Group mentoring would be required in case of group projects including classroom projects undertaken by the students, and is of particular importance in the case of industry visits and assignments. The department will assign the group mentor for each group of students. Group mentors are to be oriented about the inputs to be given to students and the monitoring to be done. Assessment of the performance of individual students in terms of their learning as well as their contribution to the group should be made. Internal conflicts and tensions within the group as may arise are to be handled by the mentor and not allowed to escalate. The mentor will mentor the group as a whole as well as its individual members for the duration of the assignment and to give feedback report.

3. Subject Mentoring. The subject mentor will be responsible for mentoring the students especially for the subject that they are teaching. The mentoring will be one to one mentoring or group mentoring based on the nature of the subject and assignments, keeping in mind the area of expertise of the faculty. Mentor will play a critical role in mentorship on account of their deeper insights into the student's academic nature and interests.

4. Peer Mentoring. A senior student may be appointed as a mentor who will advise the junior on various matters concerning assignments, conduct of mentee in classroom, course-related choices, career pathways, etc. This is to help the new student adjust to college life, the campus environment and to their role expectations as students. It would also be about building friendship, handling the pressures of college life, networking with the large student community and participating positively in the ecosystem of the campus. Feedback of the academic mentor will be taken before assigning a peer mentor. Preferably, the peer mentor may belong to similar background to help ease the transition of the mentee into the campus ethos. The peer mentors would be given orientation on their roles and responsibilities. They will be expected to report to the head of department during the semester regarding the experience of mentorship and may point to any issues which require intervention. Stipend support is provided and certificates issued on the successful completion of the mentoring activity.

5. **E-Mentoring.** Where a mentor is dedicated to answer frequently asked questions (FAQs) by students which may also be of concern to others. This type of mentoring will provide a platform where students can address issues related to generic information required by them. The e-mentor will be responsible for all communication related to the following in each department campus wise:

- Courses (majors, specialisations, electives)
- Assignments and assessments
- Career pathways
- Internships
- Projects
- FAQs related to the above

The head of department will identify an e-mentor for the above work. He/she will answer FAQs that have or are likely to arise, and will update the same. All students will be provided the details of the e-mentor, who is expected to give generic information and advice pertaining to the department. Specific questions that pertain to the individual will be redirected to the academic mentor through the concerned. The e-mentor will update the FAQ responses on an annual basis, or if there is an update or new communication.

6. **Junior Mentoring.** A junior mentor can guide in terms of innovation and the next generation skills required, latest trends and interests. This can help both together wherein they can also learn from the senior.

7. **Self-mentoring.** The student can mentor herself/himself through resources such as books, biographies, you-tube, podcasts, blogs, etc. Listen to own self. Carve out own goals and track them.

8. **Mentoring Coordinator.** Individual students with specific queries and issues related to career pathways can be sent to mentoring coordinator by departments in semester. Coordinator will mentor the students on individuated pathways. He/She will review the quality of mentoring with the academic mentor and with the subject faculty, in the departmental committee meetings as and when required. He/She will arrange for orientation to the concerned faculty mentors to enable to take on their responsibilities effectively and sensitively.

7.2.3 Assessment of Mentoring

1. **Subject Mentoring.** The faculty can document and assess the effectiveness of the mentoring as per the transaction and assessment pattern of the particular subjects.

2. **Internship.** Documentation of mentoring with specific feedback signed by both student and mentor. In case of outstation students, all mails on mentoring to be documented along with acknowledgement by student.

3. **Project.** Documentation of mentoring with specific feedback signed by both student and mentor. In case of outstation students, all emails on mentoring to be documented along with acknowledgement by student.

7.2.4 All mentoring feedback forms to be taken into account at the time of mid-term and end-term assessment to the student. Mentoring report to be given by mentoring coordinator at the end of each semester.

(i) **Academic Mentors.** Academic mentor needs to document each student's choices and feedback given by the mentor. The documentation is signed by both student and mentor and submitted to head of the department.

(ii) **E-Mentor.** Report on all communications is submitted to head of the department at the end of each semester.

(iii) **Feedback on Mentoring.** A feedback system to ensure feedback to be taken from students on all types of mentoring by the faculty every semester.

8

Inclusive Education—The Way Forward

8.1 WHAT IS INCLUSION?

UNESCO defines inclusive education as "a process of addressing and responding to the diversity of needs of all learners through increasing participation in learning, cultures and communities, and reducing exclusion within and from education. It involves changes and modifications in content, approaches, structures and strategies, with a common vision which covers all children of the appropriate age range and a conviction that it is the responsibility of the state to educate all children." Inclusive education is not a marginal issue, but is central to the achievement of high-quality education for all learners and the development of more inclusive societies.

According to UNESCO (2009), "...an 'inclusive' education system can only be created if ordinary schools become more inclusive—in other words, if they become better at educating all children in their communities" (p. 8). In India, inclusive education is mainly seen as the education of students with disabilities in regular schools. For example, the Ministry of Human Resource Development (2003) uses the following definition: "Inclusive education means all learners...with and without disabilities being able to learn together in ordinary pre-school provisions, schools, and community educational settings with an appropriate network of support services."

Inclusive education is not only about issues of input, such as access, and those related to processes such as teacher training,

- Creating links with community organisations and programmes, disabled people's organisations and parents' associations
- A flexible national curriculum
- Sufficient places and teachers availability
- Pupil-centred pedagogy where all can progress at their optimum pace
- Assessment systems made flexible to include all learners
- Specialist teachers made available to support mainstream
- Sufficient capital for building and modification
- A media and public awareness campaign to establish a rights-based approach to disability and inclusive education environments.

Radical changes are required in education systems, and in the values and principles of the people involved in delivering education. Central to an inclusive approach is a commitment to putting inclusive values into action, valuing every life equally, helping everyone feel a sense of belonging. Commitment to the right of every student with a disability to inclusive education through legal reform; policy and guidance; service delivery; attitudinal and cultural change; respect for human rights; training and support for teachers; participatory engagement with children and families is necessary. Institutes should be supported as a resource to build closer relationships with the community to address violence in and around schools.

Students, staff, parents and other partners such as police, health services, social services, faith-based groups, community recreation groups and cultural groups should all be encouraged to be involved. It requires an understanding of inclusion as an approach to education for all children that includes education policies and strategies to promote the right to access education; the right to quality education; and respect for rights within the learning environment. In addition, this approach needs to be underpinned by a broad strategic commitment across governments to create the necessary environment for ensuring the rights of children with disabilities.

8.3 DISABILITY SUPPORT SERVICE

To encourage an inclusive environment which enables students to develop their skills, knowledge and strategies to manage their own learning and to achieve their full potential through providing advice and co-ordinating support in relation to disabilities and specific learning differences promoting independent study and contributing to inclusivity within the institute. Learning managers to provide advice and co-ordinate support for disabled students. Support roles include:

- mentoring to provide assistance with planning, organizing and coping with a course of study
- to provide in studio assistance such as note taking and physical support with carrying and moving equipment
- tutors work with students to develop effective study skills
- support teachers of the hearing impaired
- offer advice before start of course
- provide an initial assessment of disability/specific learning difficulty support needs
- arrange diagnostic tests and formal needs assessments and provide advice on external funding sources for disability support
- provide support to students with short-term disabilities
- provide information, resources and advice about disabilities and specific learning difficulties to academic staff
- co-ordinate one to one support in the studio, for specialist study skills or mentoring including the opportunity to review this support on a regular basis or provide advice on alternative sources of support
- advisers are responsible for on-course support
- offer some referral information about personal care support
- support is not a substitute for the teaching of your course's academic team or self-managed study

- support to help access the learning opportunities and to assist in developing skills and strategies specific to individual needs so that they are able to work to full potential
- engaging with the adviser in order to facilitate and maintain all support needs.

9
Sustainability in Education

Some of the holistic approaches to knowledge need to include inter-disciplinarity across subjects, creative and critical thinking and systemic thinking, value explicitness and ethical concerns, solving real world problems, collaborative and participatory approaches, experiential learning, reflexive learning, etc. A sustainably literate person is one who is expected to understand sustainable ways of doing things, individually and collectively, have sufficient knowledge and skills to decide and act in a way that favours sustainability and adaptability with resilience.

Academic institutions need to abandon long-established traditions of academic isolation and become active contributors to sustainability through innovative teaching, research and outreach. Collaborative strategies should be explored as a means to keep pace with accelerated advancement and resource sharing. Integrating actions of conservation and human development, satisfying basic human needs, achieving equality and social justice for all, facilitating social self-determination and cultural diversity, managing legacy for future generations, maintaining ecological integrity, developing new technologies and product manufacturing processes are some of the goals which can lead to sustainability.

Inclusive education requires systemic measures and respect for rights within learning environments—right to respect for identity, culture and language and personal and physical integrity. The solutions should be attitudinal and cultural, environmental and organizational, and operate at international, national, regional and institute level. Inclusive education is an on-going process and a way of thinking. Student engagement needs to be embedded as a part of institutional philosophy and practice. A proper structure to accommodate students at all levels with regular monitoring and review of engagement activities need to be carried out and documented. A student engagement audit is needed to review the activities, professionals and resources and the level of the student participation.

This chapter outlines the necessity of networking and alliances of educational institutions to re-orient education towards value-based education, intercultural education, designing integrated curricula, quality education, inclusive education, and delivery of effective programs and creative engagement of students. It highlights the need for building sustainable goals and approaches for innovative education. A better connect of students with the society is required so that they can sustain and adapt, while moving along the society on the development path. The discussion involves broadly on requirement of innovative leadership and institutional reforms involving stakeholders of education, including the educators, researchers, students, parents, employers, social activists, media and government, to help formulate educational policy and programs. Networking and strategic planning in education are essential for sustainable development and capacity building in problem-based research and learning.

9.1 EDUCATION AND CULTURE

Education and culture are intimately and integrally connected. Just as culture influences education, much in the same way education also exerts a powerful influence upon the culture. Thus, whereas education culturises an individual, it preserves, transmits and develops the culture of a society. Education and culture are mutually interdependent, complementary and supplementary in all their aspects and activities. Technology, globalization, migrations, multiculturalism, and shrinking borders combine to promote a more interdependent future, in which development of a global mindset is necessary in order to live meaningfully and productively in the 21st century. One has to confront to ever-shifting social, cultural, and technological challenges. Successfully communicating with people from other cultures requires learning more than just language. The different thinking and expression patterns cause misunderstanding which leads to problems in intercultural communication. To be competent in intercultural interaction, intercultural awareness is required. This is required for intercultural sensitivity, which in turn leads to intercultural competence (Deardoff, 2004). Mostly, the teacher is not able to understand and interpret diverse cultures. Also, it can be a problem of structure. Even if the teacher knows the languages and culture, the system does not see the person as contributor to curriculum; instead it tries to develop a curriculum that prioritizes common transactional standards over contextual creative processes.

The value of self-restraint and simplicity in life and habits need to be stressed upon as part of value-based education. With utmost sincerity with which students adhered to the maxim in simple living and high thinking, the insistence upon self-discipline for the formation of proper habits and repentance develop students into excellent human beings who know how to cherish the positive values of life. These institutions will stand apart because of the democratic principles followed in student management. This, on the one hand, prevents any heart-burning and petty mindedness, on the other, leads to the development of harmony and democratic approach in the personal relationships of the students among themselves. Freedom and liberty will lead to realization of larger synthesis is which the theoretical and conventional differences are reconciled.

9.2 BUILDING COLLABORATIONS AND NETWORKING

> In democratic countries the science of associations is the mother science; the progress of all the rest depends upon the progress it has made.
>
> —*Alexis De Tocqueville*

As the traditional funding to educational institutions is shrinking, organizations are recognizing addressing common issues jointly so as to comply with the emerging challenges to education in the 21st century. Collaborations reduce duplication of cost and effort. The goal of collaboration is to bring educators, students and the stakeholders together in an atmosphere of support to systematically solve existing and emerging problems in deciphering education. Leaders must understand and develop interconnecting systems for clear communication, trust building and the sharing of human and fiscal resources. Innovations rarely occur in a vacuum. Fostering collaboration and interconnectedness is particularly important for educational institutions, as we all have similar goals that can't be achieved without one another. The constraints are the struggles of people who want to work collaboratively but who are locked into institutional structures and cultures that reinforce individualistic work

Networking is essential for pooling and exchange of information, experience and research findings. Networking is crucial for sharing of experiences, resources, theory and inspiration. New information technologies can play an essential role in community-building. Institutions of higher education have a crucial role to play in advancing the goal of a sustainable society, through their roles in both research and education. Successful efforts to increase sustainability at colleges and universities can have a large impact in the conservation of both natural and financial resources and provide an example for the larger community to help shape the values and behaviors of students. There is a possibility of sharing success stories, networking, and exploring opportunities for collaboration. Also by sharing best practices, provincially, nationally and internationally, we can provide models for adoption at all levels of the education system. Institutions need to move from bureaucratic and disciplinary structures to an organizational context that supports collaboration and foster group and cross-divisional activities. They are structured to support individual performances and hence academic organizations need redesigning.

9.3 INTER-CULTURAL COMPETENCY

Taylor defined intercultural competency as a transformative process whereby the "stranger" develops adaptive capacity, altering his or her perspective to understand and accommodate the demands of the host culture effectively. As such, intercultural competency is not a result of something, but an ongoing, individual internal process. An intercultural competent person manifests increased affective, behavioral, and cognitive abilities, such as empathy, adaptive motivation, an ability to tackle alternative perspectives, behavioral flexibility, and person-centered communication. Thus, intercultural competency can be defined as transformation of learning and a growth process where an individual's existing, often implicit, knowledge is diversified to intercultural knowledge, attitude, and behavior (Taylor, 1994).

HEIs are required to provide an environment in which students can learn the nature of global society and skills for effectively communicating with people of diverse cultures. The key to successfully facing the challenge academically is to internationalize the curriculum, understand sensitizing cultural concepts, and adaptability. Tolerance and mutual respect for other cultures and intercultural awareness can only lead to intercultural sensitivity, and both abilities will in turn lead to intercultural competence. The need is to overcome ethnocentrism and adaptability to alter the understanding and meet demands of cultural differences for better obtaining the knowledge and skills required for survival in the 21st century.

Goodwill is essential and one has to go beyond simplistic communication. Obstinate or extremist interpretation of words and behavior do not contribute positively to cross-cultural communication. Only mutual respect for diversities helps reconcile problems and reinforce good communication.

One has to learn how to deal with unexpectedness, ambiguity and otherness as well as the resulting culture bumps or culture shock. The knowledge, skills and attitudes that are necessary for successful intercultural communication have to be observed, discussed and practiced. The rapid development requires a new way of living and learning together. The terminology used for intercultural competence includes global competence, global citizenship, cross-cultural competence, international competence, intercultural effectiveness, intercultural sensitivity, etc. Some have the same general components of intercultural competence such as empathy, flexibility, cross-cultural awareness, and managing stress, while some definitions of intercultural competence specifically note other elements such as technical skills, foreign language proficiency, and situational factors.

Strong international understanding has been expressed by Indian philosophers. Sir Aurobindo was a staunch internationalist, in spite of his very emphatic expression of nationalism. Rabindranath Tagore expressed such vehement support for multicultural thinking. His creation, Shantiniketan is the concrete manifestation of the international attitude in education. Dr. S. Radhakrishnan, the Chairman of Indian Universities Commission drew attention to the need for international attitude in education. He expressed regret at the failure of the educational system to propagate feelings of internationalism and universal brotherhood. An education system should be such that it can create a new generation of individuals who believe that all human beings are brothers and that differences of caste, region, community or nation have no significance. True education is a training in internationalism. Dr. S. Radhakrishnan commented that one must make efforts for the unity of the world. We should try to create a new generation which has faith in the nobility of intellectual life, in purity, in a feeling of brotherhood towards humanity, in love and peace. There should be no national educational plan which proves an obstacle in the growth and spread of this feeling. Education must aim at making every man and woman a citizen of the world, by developing within each one such thinking, concentration, insight and intellectuality or spirituality that they can perform useful roles in life. Peace in the world can be expected only when this ideal is pursued by education in every country.

9.4 BRIDGING THE GAP

Universities provide opportunities for the meeting of artists, scientists, literary figures and scholars which creates internal understanding at a very high level and thus are the most important medium of propagating international education at a very high level and propagating international education. Many institutions of the UNO, particularly UNESCO, are engaged in directly and consciously promoting international understanding and the growth of cross-cultural feeling. Participation in these programs can help achieve the desired goals. There is a need for scrutinizing the ideological basis of higher education, drawing from these ideologies, identifying the cornerstones of intercultural competencies and proposing an adequate model.

Intercultural competitions/festivals bring people into contact. Exhibitions also play an important part in promoting international understanding, because it helps to acquaint people with the art and culture of different regions/countries. Films give a lot of information. Besides, it also encourages the feeling that human beings are the same everywhere in their happiness, pain, pleasure, problems, joys and sorrow. Radio and TV also help understand life in other parts of the world. Literature, which is almost available in every country helps in increasing acquaintance with life as it is lived in different parts. Certain books compile the stories of lives, character, interesting incidents and surprising objects which help.

Inter-culturalism should also indicate student learning and attitudes. Institutions that are serious about its effect on students should take a closer look at learning goals, course content, pedagogy, campus life, enrollment pattern, and institutional policies and practices to get a more complete picture of their success (Engberg and Green, 2002). Schools and classrooms, generally, are not organized to accommodate diversity. They assume that all children bring a similar socialization, one that corresponds closely to the experiences of dominant groups. Students who enter schools with ways of learning that differ from the expected norm often are seen as deficient. Culturally responsible educators must believe that the students are capable of learning and hold high expectations from each one. Critical thinking and evaluation of one's own activities in an international perspective and respect for other people, culture and values remain a cardinal element of all education. Humanity is the true religion of human beings, while all the great religions are only different forms of it. All great religions have placed great stress upon the quality of human beings. Faith in humanity and love for all human beings irrespective of the country is necessary.

The entire climate and culture of departments, schools, or colleges of education as well as the college or university campus and cooperating schools should radiate a consistent, pervasive, and comprehensive appreciation for and promotion of cultural diversity. Multi-culturalism must convey these in the way they relate to students and colleagues and in how they ground the pedagogical concepts, principles, theories, and strategies they teach. This commitment is also conveyed through lecture series, awards for promotion of cultural diversity and educational equality for marginalized ethnic and social groups. Evidence from research and wisdom from best practice points out that students should understand and implement a multicultural perspective in their classes and during their field experiences, such a perspective should permeate the entire curriculum including courses taken outside their schools, departments, and colleges of education.

Academic programs do not operate in isolation and are a part of institutions of higher education which have their own particular histories, policies, and cultures. These policies and procedures include recruitment, support, and retention of faculty, staff, and students of color, a multicultural core curriculum, service to a diverse community, and numerous multicultural experiences for students and educators. The goal of a multicultural education program is to help teachers become change agents who can impact power relationships through curriculum, instructional practices, and individual and collective action towards more just personal and structural relationships.

9.5 VALUE ORIENTATION

Value education develops our wisdom, and gives us the power to differentiate between right and wrong. Today, value education is the prime need of the universe for developing of the feeling of universal brotherhood. The scope of value education is wide, and nobody can ignore its importance. We need the education that relates human beings with the feeling that we are one and so we should respect each other. A better connect of students with the society is required so that they can sustain and adapt, while moving along the society on the development path. Value-based education and a better connect with other educational institutions and peers are also needed to become resilient and effectively overcome difficulties.

Human being is the most evolved creation amongst all the living beings. His/her life possesses meaning beyond self-protection. They have to make their own destiny guided by certain values which are illuminating forces of their life processes. The great centres of learning like Nalanda, Vikramshila, Jagaddala, Nadia, Odantpuri and Vallabhi in India imbued the rising generations with the traditions of a great society who, for centuries sustained on such human values which nurtured free minds and urged them to full and fair enquiry which brought wisdom into human affairs. The unorthodox and liberal approach advocated an all-encompassing spirit of universal brotherhood which knows no boundaries of nationalities, faiths or sects. Other values highly cherished by educationists were self-sacrificing asceticism, self-concentration which developed moral sentiments and character. Acknowledging that the personality of youngsters formed the backbone of the whole value system of society, it was sought to be developed by these universities by eulogizing the feeling of self-respect, encouraging the sense of self-confidence inculcating the virtue of self-restraint and fostering the powers of judgement.

The entire system was based on the principle of personal touch and warmth. Rules of discipline that were prescribed for the students were laid down not so much for the purpose of prohibiting from doing undesirable acts as with the object of forming good and valuable habits. Rules were framed which developed them into strong and hard persons and prepared them for the long struggles in life with determined wit and great enduring power. The self-confidence of the students was fostered by regular meetings, discussions and debates between scholars and students at regular intervals. The friction of the best minds was the best possible means of developing and sharpening the wits and self-confidence of the participants. It was an ideal platform for the students to broaden their knowledge base, to correct incorrect orientations and thus move forward towards personal and thereby social betterment.

9.6 CULTURE OF SUSTAINABILITY

The interlinked strategies proposed for the promotion and implementation of education for sustainable development in many discussion forums are advocacy and vision-building, consultation and ownership, partnership and networks, capacity-building and training, research and innovation, information and communication technologies, monitoring and evaluation. Creating a culture of sustainability, education approaches to fostering sustainable behavior among the community and building systems and awareness for sustainability. While student and faculty exchange is a common practice nowadays, a library consortium provides a way for its members to conduct business in a comparative manner. The basic premise of consortia is that its members can collectively achieve more than what they can achieve as individual institutions. The consortium constantly monitors international developments in this area and liaise with agencies to bring the best possible consortium-based solutions to its members.

The syllabi should include painting, literature, music, typical of different countries, overcoming narrow mindedness, include contributions of great leaders of the world, the rights and duties to international community, and encourage pen friendship. Stress on humanity and world citizenship is required. The teaching should not only concentrate upon the differences but also on similarities so that sympathy for all nations and nationals is awakened in the minds. The educator having an international viewpoint can inspire through conversations, ideas, training and examples. International contacts among scientists, scholars, literary figures, teachers, doctors, etc., and mutual exchange of scholars and learned people helps. Every national plan of education must make a specific provision for developing international feeling. Effective methods to assess intercultural competence in educational institutions should be developed.

Cultural differences are impossible to avoid. The key to successfully face the challenge academically is to help students understand globalization, sensitizing cultural concepts, have self-perception and emotional and cognitive acquisitions, in order to reach a high level of empathy, govern their performance and emotions in working and in living with people from other cultures by increasing their adaptability, and adopt a changed way of perceiving and behaving, so that they can improve their social performance. The students should be valued and revered not only in the country but in foreign lands where they become harbingers and torch-bearers of their culture and civilization. They should develop into physically, mentally, emotionally and spiritually sound human beings and work for the emancipation of the society. Celebrating diversity is the key to sustainable literacy. Finally, it is about Retain—what is of value, Revise—what might need modification, Reject—what we need to abandon, Renew—what new ideas, concepts, principles, methodologies, working methods, pedagogies, etc. are needed.

The fundamentals of education are to educate the individual as a free individual; to understand and use critical thinking skills and to educate the individual as a part of society. Through education, knowledge must continually be renewed by ceaseless effort, if it is not to be lost. The hands on and practice based education and a multi-disciplinary approach, is must for holistic learning and developing resilience.

10

Summary, Conclusions and Suggestions

With the rapid development of society and economy there is a demand for professionalism in education which has become the common understanding progressively. It is a process during which the teachers and students learn from each other, explore the world of new knowledge and develop together, and also one in which the ideal, ethics and emotion of profession and the sense of social responsibility. Continuous improvement approaches are needed so that institutions can more rapidly respond to change and input from professional, organizational and industry sources. The major components for developing a system for this are transparency in providing information, approach to teaching, delivery of teaching, outcomes of teaching and learning and student engagement in decision making and governance.

HE, research and innovation play a crucial role in supporting social cohesion, economic growth and global competitiveness. As one strives to become increasingly knowledge-based, HE is an essential component of socio-economic and cultural development. An increasing demand for skills and competencies makes HE to lay new paths. There are increasingly diverse individual experiences available in HE and responding to this and growing expectations requires a fundamental shift. A student-centered approach to learning and teaching, embracing flexible learning paths and recognizing competencies gained outside formal curricula is necessary. HEIs themselves also become more diverse in their missions, mode of educational provision and cooperation, including growth of internationalization, digital learning and new forms of delivery. The role of quality assurance is crucial in supporting HE systems and institutions in responding to these changes while ensuring that academics in the priority.

HE aims to fulfil multiple purposes; including preparing students for active citizenship, for their future, supporting their personal development, creating a broad advanced knowledge base and stimulating research and innovation. Quality assurance needs to take into account these different perspectives. Quality assurance should ensure a learning environment in which the content of programmes, learning opportunities and facilities are fit for purpose. At the heart of all quality assurance activities are the twin purposes of accountability and enhancement. Quality assurance and quality enhancement are inter-related. They can support the development of a quality culture that is embraced by all, from the students and academic staff to the institutional leadership and management. The term 'quality assurance' thus describes all activities within the continuous improvement cycle.

The nationalistic and internationalist feelings need to be synthesized in contemporary education for which peaceful coexistence and active co-operation is important. The objectives of education, syllabus and methods of teaching need to promote internationalism. From time immemorial, there have been examples of the many benefits of collaboration. Indeed, innovations rarely occur in a vacuum. Fostering collaboration and interconnectedness is particularly important for educational institutions, as we all have similar goals that can't be achieved without one another. The organizations and institutions which can form a network are academic institutions, research institutions, agencies and institutions of central/state governments and non-governmental organizations. Some of the challenges to education for sustainable development are institutionalizing sustainability, creating a culture of sustainability, connecting cognitive and creative arenas, performing collaborative research, collaborative peer group networking, competencies to develop strategies to work on sustainable development in future careers.

10.1 INTERNAL QA

Quality assurance policies to be effective should reflect the relationship between research and learning and teaching and take account of both the national context in which the institution operates, the institutional context and its strategic approach. It encourages joint responsibility, academic integrity and freedom and is vigilant against academic fraud, guarding against intolerance or discrimination and involvement of external stakeholders. The system ensures that the programmes are designed with overall objectives that are in line with the institutional strategy and have explicit intended learning outcomes. Student-centered learning and teaching plays an important role in stimulating students' motivation, self-reflection and engagement in the learning process. This means careful consideration of the design and delivery of study programmes and the assessment of outcomes. It considers the importance of assessment for the students' progression and their future careers. Internships and other periods of the programme that are not spent in the institution but that allow the student to gain experience in an area related to their studies are included.

The procedures for admission, recognition and completion, particularly when students are mobile within and across higher education systems should fit the purpose. It is important that they are consistent and transparent. Conditions and support that are necessary for students to make progress in their academic career is in the best interest of the students, programmes, institutions and systems. Institutions should have processes and tools to collect, monitor and act on information on student progression. Fair recognition of HE qualifications, periods of study and prior learning, including the recognition of non-formal and informal learning, are essential components for ensuring the students' progress in their studies, while promoting mobility. Quality of staff and a supportive environment helps in effective operations.

Institutions provide a range of resources to assist student learning, which vary from physical resources such as libraries, study facilities and IT infrastructure to human support in the form of tutors, counselors and other advisers. The needs of diverse student population, student-centred learning and flexible modes of learning and teaching are taken into account when allocating, planning and providing the learning resources and student support. Support activities and facilities may be organized in a variety of ways depending on the institutional context. However, the internal quality assurance ensures that all resources are fit for purpose, accessible, and that students are informed about the services available to them. In delivering support services the role of support staff is crucial and therefore they need to be qualified and trained.

Institutions provide information about their activities, including the programmes they offer and selection criteria, intended learning outcomes, awards, teaching, learning and assessment procedures, pass percentage, learning opportunities available to students and graduate employment information. This information is useful for prospective and current students as well as for graduates, other stakeholders and the public. Regular monitoring, review and revision of study programmes, aim to ensure a supportive and effective learning environment for students.

More flexibility in the academic programmes and more options for the students to not only make the initial choice but also to make a mid-course change if they are unable to sustain in the course they opted for.

The emphasis should be more on assessing the all-round development of students for which reforms in the educational and assessment procedures are necessary. Quality education could come only if there were quality teachers who were good communicators, who could win the confidence of students and who were approachable and generally available for students. Quality in education would become apparent if the curriculum had adaptability and was designed to address the all-round development of the students. Students need to be provided with better access to information. Co-curricular activities needed to facilitate the all-round development of students were being ignored at the moment, and these activities were only seen during the annual college festivals or youth festivals. Quality of education should not be linked only to marks.

It is important that the spirit of learning be emphasized. Students are apprehensive that candid opinion expressed in the feedback could invite victimization and punitive action. Though it is made clear that the student need not disclose his or her identity in the feedback form, yet these apprehensions indicated a lack of mutual trust. It is a wonder if feedback could have any impact under such circumstances. The assessment teams visiting the institute should interact with students separately and the feedback from students should be considered.

10.2 EXTERNAL QA

Quality assurance does not end with the external feedback or report or its follow-up process within the institution. Therefore, institutions ensure that the progress made since the last external quality assurance activity is taken into consideration when preparing for the next one. Quality assurance is based on the institutions' responsibility for the quality of their programmes and other provision; therefore it is important that external quality assurance recognises and supports institutional responsibility for quality assurance. At the core of external quality assurance is the wide range of expertise provided by peer experts, who contribute to the work of the agency through input from various perspectives, including those of institutions, academics, students and employers/professional practitioners. Independence of the experts needs to be ensured. The involvement of international experts in external quality assurance is desirable as it adds a further dimension to the development and implementation of processes.

External quality assurance and in particular its outcomes have a significant impact on institutions and programmes that are evaluated and judged. In the interests of equity and reliability, outcomes of external quality assurance are based on pre-defined and published criteria, which are interpreted consistently and are evidence-based. Depending on the external quality assurance system, outcomes may take different forms, for example, recommendations, judgments or formal decisions. The report by the experts is the basis for the institution's follow-up action of the external evaluation and it provides information to society regarding the activities of an institution. In order for the report to be used as the basis for action to be taken, it needs to be clear and concise, with evidence, analysis and findings, conclusions, features of good practice and recommendations. The institution should be given an opportunity to point out errors before the report is finalized. The institute can appeal against the outcomes of the process, where it can demonstrate that the outcome is not based on sound evidence, that criteria have not been correctly applied or that the processes have not been consistently implemented.

The goals and objectives of the quality assurance activities be described and published along with the nature of interaction between the agencies and relevant stakeholders in higher education. The expertise in the agency may be increased by including international members in committees.

A periodic external review will help the agency to reflect on its policies and activities. It provides a means for assuring the agency and its stakeholders that it continues to adhere to the principles.

10.3 CHANGING PARADIGMS

A big focus was on the need to improve the career prospects of India's younger generation through better education. A huge budget is allotted for enhancing skills of youth. Creating opportunities for youth to acquire education and skills that would get them decent jobs or create self-employment with decent incomes is an overarching goal, it was stated. The rising demand and shrinking fiscal space has given rise to the thinking of inviting Public Private Partnership (PPP) in the administration and financing of HE. PPP is the new dimension of the joint responsibility for the development of the education sector by non-public resources. The sustainability of any sector depends on the viability of costs and benefits and PPP in education has come to flourish on the principle of cost and benefit sharing. It is equally important to note the required fundamental transformation at both system level and at institutional level in HE. Effective financial management at institutional level is mandatory. The challenge to public policy on higher education in India remains to combine private providers with continuing responsibility of government to guide, regulate, monitor, with a view to strike a balance between equity and efficiency.

As a result of dwindling government grants and with the government even imposing cuts on the committed grants, resulting lack of requisite and regular faculty, inadequate development of infrastructure and facilities, lack of latest equipment, etc. In order to offset the financial crunch, the universities are looking for alternative non-governmental resources for their smooth functioning. Fee hike has been the easiest way adopted to deal with financial crisis. Along with hike in student fees, the universities are continuously raising other fees and charges like prices for forms and prospectus, examination fees, migration fee, etc. Introduction of self-financing institutions have been other significant measures resorted to by the universities. These are shifting focus from fundamental research and teaching basic sciences and social sciences to professional courses. Besides, the conduct of entrance tests for different courses is proving to be a big source of revenue for the universities.

Other measures adopted by universities to cope with financial crunch have been developing collaborations with industries, consultancy, alumni associations, getting donations from individuals and institutions, sponsorships from corporate houses, commercial use of facilities, allowing commercial advertisement in the campus, etc. Besides, the universities have been adopting austerity measures especially not filling the teaching and non-teaching posts on regular basis. In the face of universities being engaged in resource generating and cost cutting exercises, new paradigms of their financial management have started emerging.

The role of a teacher includes being a process facilitator, counsellor, assessor, researcher, technologist, designer and a manager of learning. The competencies required by teachers include awareness about the student requirement, knowledge of evaluation, IT, new developments, etc. An educational leader may need basic skills like working together, understanding human behavior, and vision for the future, motivation and development of key competencies. Some of the essential traits required in a leader are striving for excellence, communicating effectively, creativity, maintaining human relations and delegating efficiently. The objective of higher education, make it an instrument of producing trained competence with sharpened problem-solving capability and revive confidence in the system of higher education.

10.4 NEED TO PROMOTE ENTREPRENEURSHIP

There is a need for creating an educational system that highlights the importance of entrepreneurship. In the present context, the education system has to be designed in a way that produces large number of employment generators and not just employment seekers, according to Late Prof. Abdul Kalam, former President of India. To achieve this, there was the need for a strategy that could make education more attractive, skill oriented and employment generating. The country's education system should prepare students to get oriented towards setting up enterprises which can give them creativity, freedom and ability to generate wealth. The curriculum should provide market research support to students for selection of right products and guide young entrepreneurs through the incubation period till they stand on their own.

Technology can affect fundamental changes in the ground rules of economic competitiveness. Science is linked to technology through applications. Technology is linked to economy and environment through manufacture of knowledge products. Economy and environment are linked to technology, which promotes prosperity to the society. We have to use innovation to generate high value added products for becoming a global player, says Prof. Kalam.

10.5 THE TALENT GAP

The significance of the developing nations is rising as the major growth driver. There are several challenges on socio-economic front acting as potential growth disrupters. Education is one such key issue being faced by all the emerging countries, including India. Although the Indian Government is making considerable budgetary allocations for education expenditure, the quality of education still remains one of the major concerns. While the country is home to a considerable number of engineering, medical and management schools, the industry by and large suffers from the talent crunch. Ensuring access to quality education for all, in particular for the poor and rural population, is central to the economic and social development of India. CII and the Boston Consulting Group have pointed out in a report that the mismatch between educational standard and sustainability for employment will result in a 'talent gap.' According to reports 25% of technical and 10% of non-technical people are employable. Any initiative to arrest and reverse the rapidly deteriorating situation will have necessarily to begin with educational institutions. There is, in fact, plenty that can be done even within the existing pattern of education and academic and professional course content to raise the level of awareness and proficiency of the students.

The recognition of the organization as a system and the work done within the organization must be seen as an ongoing process. Quality management must be applied to correct the flaws in the system that makes individuals to fail. Since systems are made up of processes, the improvements made in the quality of those processes largely determine the quality of the resulting product. In the new paradigm of learning, continual improvement of learning processes based on learning outcomes replaces the outdated "teach and test" mode.

Bibliography

Arcaro, Jerome S. (1997). *Quality in Education—An Implementation Handbook*, Vanity Books International, New Delhi.

Astin, A.W. (1984). Student Involvement: A Developmental Theory for Higher Education. *Journal of College Student Development*, Volume 40, No. 5. Baltimore: The Johns Hopkins University Press.

Bell, J. (1999). *Doing Your Research Project*, third edition, Buckingham, Open University Press, 128.

Bishop, G. (1989). *Alternate Strategies for Education*, Macmillan Publishers Ltd., London.

Davis, N., Cho, M.O. and Hagenson, L. (2005). Intercultural Competence and the Role of Technology in Teacher Education. *Contemporary Issues in Technology and Teacher Education,* 4 (4).

Deardorff, D. (2004). In Search of Intercultural Competence. *International Educator*, 13 (2), pp. 13-15.

Denison, D., Hooijberg, R. and Quinn, R. (1995). Paradox and performance: Toward a theory of behavioral complexity in managerial leadership. *Organization Science,* 6, pp. 524-40.

Deshmukh, Vijaya (Ed.) (2011). *Education in the Emerging India*. New Delhi: Atlantic Publishers and Distributors Pvt. Ltd.

———. (2012). *Education for Human Resource Development.* New Delhi: Atlantic Publishers and Distributors Pvt. Ltd.

———. (2012). *Winds of Reform in Indian Education.* New Delhi: Atlantic Publishers and Distributors Pvt. Ltd.

———. (2006). Collaboration & Networking—A Key to Sustainable Development in Asia & Pacific regions. In: *10th UNESCO-APEID International Conference—Learning Together for Tomorrow: Education for Sustainable Development,* Bangkok: UNESCO.

———. (2007). Role of Higher Education in building Intercultural Competence. In: *4th International Conference on Intercultural Communication Competence (ICICC). Building bridges among educational communities: World Class Practices in Higher Education.* Mexico: ICICC.

———. (2010). Greening the campuses to promote sustainable development. In: *Working Group on Global Warming Conference & Expo 10 (WGGW Conference & Expo 10).* London: WGGW.

———. (2010). Trends in Indian Higher Education System. In: *International Education and Development Conference—INTED 2010,* Valencia: INTED.

———. (2011) Managing diversity in classrooms. *41st ISTD National Convention Towards Cutting Edge HR Strategy—Issues, Prospects and Challenges.* Indian Society for Training & Development (ISTD), Kota.

Elfert, M. (2015). Rethinking Education—Towards a global common good? *UNESCO, the Faure Report, the Delors Report, and the Political Utopia of Lifelong Learning, European Journal of Education,* 50 (1), pp. 88-100.

Engberg, D. and Green, M. (2002). *Promising Practices: Spotlighting Excellence in Comprehensive Internationalization.* Washington, DC: American Council on Education.

Gauthier de Beco (2014). The right to inclusive education according to Article 24 of the UN convention on the rights of persons with disabilities: Background, requirements and (remaining) questions. *Netherlands Quarterly of Human Rights,* Vol. 32/3.

Gretchen, M. and J. Jordan (2000). Cross Cultural Competency & Multicultural Teacher Education. *Review of Educational Research,* 70(1), pp. 3-24.

Indian Higher Education Accreditation System (NAAC Manual).

Kanter, Rosabeth Moss (1993). Can Schools be managed Like Business? *He School Administrator*, No. 2, Vol. 50, p. 64.

M. Chrzanowski, E. Nawarecki (ed.) (CAEE' 97), Vol. 2, pp. 156-64 (AGH Krakow), Quality Assurance in Higher Education Zbigniew Mrozek, Osei Adjei, Ali Mansour (*Proc. of 4-th Int. Conf. Computer Aided Engineering Education*).

Madhu Parhar, *University News*, November 11-17, 2002, Vol. 40, No. 45 pp. 5-6.

McCartt, A. and Rohrbaugh, J. (1989). Evaluating group decision support system effectiveness: A performance study of decision conferencing. *Decision Support Systems, 5*, pp. 243-53.

———. (1995). Managerial openness to change and the introduction of GDSS: Explaining initial success and failure in decision conferencing. *Organization Science,* 6(5), pp. 569-84.

Miles, M.B. and Huberman, A.M. *Qualitative Data Analysis* (2 edition), Thousand Oaks, CA, Sage, 1994.

Mitchell, V. (1996). Assessing the reliability and validity of questionnaires: an empirical example, *Journal of Applied Management Studies*, 5:2, pp. 199-207.

N.T. Khobragade and Sunita Sanganeria, *University News*, July 19-25, 2004, Vol. 42, No. 29, p. 23.

Nachmias, C. and Nachmias, D., *Research Methods in Social Sciences*, Australia: Edward Arnold, 1985.

Pallant, J. (2001). SPSS Survival Manual, Buckingham, Open University Press.

Publications by Quality Assurance Agency, UK.

Quality Assurance in US education system.

Quality Assurance in Australian Higher Education.

Quinn, R. and Rohrbaugh, J. (1983). A Spatial Model of Effectiveness Criteria: Towards a Competing Values approach to organizational analysis. *Management Science,* 29, pp 363-77.

Rieser, R. (2012). Implementing Inclusive Education: A Commonwealth Guide to Implementing Article 24 of the UN Convention on the Rights of Persons with Disabilities, Second Edition, London: Commonwealth Secretariat.

Sanchez, A., Gandon, R., Rey, M.J., and Carrera, E. *Quality Assurance in Higher Education.*

Sharma, Umesh and Das Ajay (2015). Inclusive education in India: Past, Present and Future. *Support for Learning*, Volume 30. Number 1, pp. 55-68.

Singh, S.K. (2012). Quality Education and Human Development. In Deshmukh, Vijaya (Ed.), *Education for Human Resource Development.* New Delhi: Atlantic Publishers and Distributors Pvt. Ltd.

Singh, Shailaja (2011). "Quality Crises in Higher Education in India" in Deshmukh, Vijaya (Ed.), *Education in the Emerging India*. New Delhi: Atlantic Publishers Distributors Pvt. Ltd.

Snehi, Neeru (2012). Improving Quality of Teaching-Learning in Higher Education: Constructivist Learning Approach in Deshmukh, Vijaya (Ed.), *Winds of Reform in Indian Education.* New Delhi: Atlantic Publishers and Distributors Pvt. Ltd.

European Association of Institutions in Higher Education (EURASHE) (2015). Standards & Guidelines for Quality Assurance in the European Higher Education Area, EURASHE, Brussels.

Sterling, S. (2014). Learning to learn for sustainability in higher education: Making a difference. In: *Education for Sustainable Development (ESD)*. [online] London. London Regional Centre of Expertise (LRCE). Available at: http://www.slideshare.net/4allofus/esd-london-conference [Accessed on 28.1.2016].

Stier, J. (2006). Internationalization, intercultural communication and intercultural competence. *Journal of Intercultural Communication*, 11, pp. 1-12.

Student Engagement. UK Quality Code for Higher Education. Part B. Assuring and Enhancing Academic Quality.

Sutanu Bhattacharya and Ratnabali Banerjee, *University News*, December 2-8, 2002, Vol. 40, No. 48, p. 1.

Taylor, C. (1994). *Multiculturalism: Examining the Politics of Recognition*. Princeton: Princeton University Press. pp. 37-38, 44, 51.

The Quality Assurance Agency for Higher Education. (2012). *Institutional Review of Higher Education-Institutions in England and Northern Ireland, A handbook for higher education providers. Second edition*. Gloucester: QAA.

The Quality Assurance Agency for Higher Education. (2015). *Higher Education Review Handbook—A handbook for universities and colleges with access to funding from HEFCE or DEL undergoing review in 2015-16*. Gloucester: QAA.

The Quality Assurance Agency for Higher Education (QAA) (2018). UK Quality Code for Higher Education. QAA, UK.

The Quality Assurance Agency for Higher Education. (2015). *Higher Education Review Handbook*, Gloucester: QAA.

The UK Quality Code for Higher Education: A Brief Guide.

The UK Quality Code for Higher Education, Quality Assurance Agency for Higher Education, 2014, Gloucester.

UNICEF (2011). The Right of Children with Disabilities to Education: A Rights-Based Approach to Inclusive Education. Geneva: UNICEF Regional Office for Central and Eastern Europe and the Commonwealth of Independent States (CEECIS).

Wright, B. (2009). Evaluating the strengths and weaknesses of group decision-making processes: A competing values approach. *Group Facilitation Fundamentals of Management*, Boston: Houghton Mifflin Co.

Zbigniew, Mrozek, Adjei, Osei., and Mansour, Ali (2018).Quality Assurance In Higher Education. In Chrzanowski, M., and Nawarecki, E. (Ed.), *4th International Conference—*

Computer Aided Engineering Education (Vol. 2, pp. 156-64), Krakow: AGH.

Zuboff, S. (1988). *In the Age of the Smart Machine: The Future of Work and Power*. Butterworth-Hienemann, Oxford.

Websites Accessed between September 10, 2016 to December 31, 2017

www.qaa.ac.uk/AssuringStandardsAndQuality/

www.qaa.ac.uk/reviews-and-reports/how-we-review-higher-education

www.qaa.ac.uk/publications/information-and-guidance/publication?PubID=181

www.qaa.ac.uk/about-us/glossary

www.qaa.ac.uk/publications/information-and-guidance/publication?PubID=171

www.qaa.ac.uk/assuring-standards-and-quality/the-quality-code/quality-code-part-c

www.qaa.ac.uk/assuring-standards-and-quality/the-quality-code/quality-code-part-c

www.qaa.ac.uk/publications/information-and-guidance/publication?PubID=179

Websites accessed in January 2018

www.guni-rmies.net/observatory/bp.php?id=65

crs.uvm.edu/nnco/collab/wellness.html

Index

Note: f and t refer to figures and tables respectively.

J

K

L

M

T